Enough
Already

ALSO BY ALAN COHEN

Are You as Happy as Your Dog?
Dare to Be Yourself
A Deep Breath of Life*
A Daily Dose of Sanity*
Don't Get Lucky, Get Smart
The Dragon Doesn't Live Here Anymore
Handle with Prayer*
Happily Even After*
Have You Hugged a Monster Today?
How Good Can it Get?
I Had It All the Time
Joy Is My Compass*
Lifestyles of the Rich in Spirit*
Linden's Last Life*
Looking In for Number One
My Father's Voice
The Peace That You Seek
Relax into Wealth
Rising in Love*
Setting the Seen
Why Your Life Sucks and What You Can Do about It
Wisdom of the Heart*

*Available from Hay House

Please visit:

Hay House USA: **www.hayhouse.com**®
Hay House Australia: **www.hayhouse.com.au**
Hay House UK: **www.hayhouse.co.uk**
Hay House South Africa: **www.hayhouse.co.za**
Hay House India: **www.hayhouse.co.in**

Enough
Already

The Power of
Radical Contentment

ALAN COHEN

HAY HOUSE, INC.
Carlsbad, California • New York City
London • Sydney • Johannesburg
Vancouver • Hong Kong • New Delhi

Published and distributed in the United States by: Hay House, Inc.: www .hayhouse.com® • *Published and distributed in Australia by:* Hay House Australia Pty. Ltd.: www.hayhouse.com.au • *Published and distributed in the United Kingdom by:* Hay House UK, Ltd.: www.hayhouse.co.uk • *Published and distributed in the Republic of South Africa by:* Hay House SA (Pty), Ltd.: www.hayhouse.co.za • *Distributed in Canada by:* Raincoast: www.raincoast.com • *Published in India by:* Hay House Publishers India: www.hayhouse.co.in

Cover design: Julie Davison • *Interior design:* Riann Bender

Library of Congress Cataloging-in-Publication Data

Cohen, Alan.
  Enough already : the power of radical contentment / Alan Cohen. -- 1st ed.
    p. cm.
  ISBN 978-1-4019-3520-7 (tradepaper : alk. paper)
  1. Contentment. 2. Attitude (Psychology) 3. Conduct of life. I. Title.
  BJ1533.C7C62 2012
  178--dc23
                              2011038499

Tradepaper ISBN: 978-1-4019-3520-7
Digital ISBN: 978-1-4019-3521-4

15 14 13 12   4 3 2 1
1st edition, February 2012

Printed in the United States of America

To my beloved parents, Robert and Jeane Cohen, who taught me that there is always enough of everything because there is always enough love.

Contents

Introduction

At a time when many people are worried about money, the divorce rate is soaring, politicians are being indicted, new poisons in food are exposed daily, natural disasters ravage the planet, wars despoil nations, and fear of terrorism has forced decent people to undress to board an airplane, the prospect of contentment seems like a bad joke or naïve fantasy. If someone asked you, "How are you?" and you answered, "I am content," the other person would probably raise an eyebrow and wonder if you were on drugs, living in denial, or had attended too many self-help seminars. In times as difficult as ours, contentment seems radical, even heretical: "How dare you be happy when so many things are going wrong . . . or could . . . or will?"

Yet contentment is not a bank balance, marital status, or pot of gold you reach at the end of the rainbow. It is a choice you make, an attitude you step into, a state of being that runs deeper than conditions. It is more available than impossible. Can you and I find a way to be at peace with ourselves and our lives right now, even before the mortgage is paid, we resolve our differences with our ex, or global warming is offset?

I have wanted many things in my life, and I still do. It had always seemed that I would be happier if I found my soul mate, lived in a bigger house, saw my book on the bestseller list, or toted the latest-generation iPad. Then I met a man who turned my belief system upside down. Shin-ichiro Terayama is a Japanese physicist who radiates joy more brilliantly than any soul I have ever met. He wears a perpetual smile and lights a room simply by entering it. I have never known someone so genuinely happy.

When Shin was diagnosed with terminal cancer, he was catapulted into deep soul-searching. He went to a Japanese garden and considered what would make his life meaningful, whether he lived one more day or another 40 years. His answer was: *to be grateful for everyone and everything*—including his cancer, as a wake-up call. From that day on, Shin said "Thank you" for every event and experience that showed up in and around him. Within a few months, the cancer disappeared. That was 25 years ago. Now Shin teaches others to find health and happiness by practicing the lost art of appreciation.

The Talmud asks: "Who is rich?" It answers: "He who is content with his lot." Upon hearing that, the negative mind might go to: *What if I were consigned to a wheelchair in a flea-bitten apartment, stuck with someone I hate, wearing thrift-store clothes, and eating dollar fast foods for dinner? I'm supposed to be happy <u>there?</u>* But think of the word *lot*. You are not given a little. You are given a lot. Only the fearful mind goes to catastrophic fantasies. The spirit within you knows that you deserve good things. If life has taken good care of you thus far, do you really believe it would stop now? And would the hand of love not bless you whatever turn your life takes? Could your life take more and more turns for the better?

Content means "to contain." You contain what you seek. It is in you, as you. No thing and no one outside you can give you or make you more than you already are. The treasure you seek, you already own. The treasure you seek, you already *are*.

Contentment does not mean complacency—lazily lying back and saying, "I will just accept what I have and never ask for more." True joy calls for you to appreciate what you have *and* reach for greater: to be happy *and* hungry. It is natural and healthy to want to grow, expand, advance, achieve, and discover more about who you are and what life has to offer—as Thoreau posited, "to live deep and suck all the marrow of life." A mature sense of happiness embraces all that you are *and* want, and moves beyond settling . . . into adventure.

Enough Already can also mean refusing to accept any situation not in harmony with your well-being.

We have all engaged in relationships, business situations, and living arrangements that demean us or lack integrity. Upon recognizing that we have sold out to fit in, we must say no to what does not serve us so we can make space for what does.

You cannot afford to settle for any situation that dampens your spirit. When you discover you have "detoured," you must do whatever it takes to return to the path of joy. Putting your foot down is a prerequisite to stepping ahead.

The sage Sri Nisargadatta stated, "In my world all is well." In what world did *he* live? Was it the one we see on the news, or was he watching a broadcast the rest of us are missing? Can we take up residence in the domain he described? Can we experience wellness even before the economy turns around, our spouse understands us, or wars come to an end?

Let's take that adventure together. This is not simply a journey into getting more. It is a journey into having more and being more, beginning by claiming the riches you already own and *are*.

We are about to leave behind burdens of loss, lack, or abandonment . . . and find the higher ground of plenty.

Enough already. Let's do it.

A Few Notes
to the Reader

You can journey through these chapters in linear fashion, one after another, or you can pick and choose the order in which you read, according to your intuition. This book is organized holographically, meaning that every chapter and section relates to the theme like spokes radiating from the center of a wheel, rather than one domino falling after another. All truths are connected to each other, like facets of a diamond. If you follow any one to the center, you will join with all the rest.

My mentor taught a technique of creative thinking based on writing down a core idea in the middle of a sheet of paper and then spontaneously noting all ideas relating to the central one, like satellites revolving around a planet. This method of free association engenders more abundant ideas than a linear method of organization. In this book, the theme "You can have enough because you are enough, you deserve enough, and enough is always available" constitutes the core lesson, and every sentence and chapter illuminates the central principle from a unique angle.

All of the anecdotes contained herein are true. I experienced them directly, or they were told to me by individuals who experienced them firsthand. In some cases, I have changed the names or identifying details to honor the privacy of the individual. In a few cases, I amalgamated several like stories for the sake of clarity and brevity.

If you have read any of my other work, you may notice a few illustrative examples carried over from my previous writings. This is by conscious choice. While as a rule I do not repeat illustrations, in a few instances the ideas are so relevant to the theme that I felt that including them would be far more helpful than leaving them out. In addition, when I previously recorded these ideas, they were in an elementary or seed form. Since that time I have fleshed them out with greater depth and applications. So in the interest of expanding your awareness of these principles, I have chosen to include them, and I hope you will find them even more illuminating.

1

Enough Already

*It is not our circumstances which create our
discontent or contentment. It is us.*

— **VIVIAN GREENE**

I was having dinner with Dr. Wayne Dyer when the subject of money came up. "I don't need any more money," Wayne told me in a matter-of-fact way. "I have enough money."

Well, sure you do, I jealously thought. *You have a ton of books on the bestseller list, and you make umpteen-thousand dollars for a lecture.*

As I considered Wayne's statement, however, I realized that it offered a brilliant teaching. Wayne Dyer has enough money because he chooses to regard what he has as enough. His sense of enough is not based on a number. It is based on his willingness to feel satisfied. I know people who have a lot more money than Dr. Dyer, and they never have enough. I also know people who have very little money, and they feel rich. Wealth and poverty are not external conditions. They are states of mind.

Since that conversation, I have practiced seeing life through the eyes of supply rather than lack, appreciation rather than complaint, ease rather than struggle. I have discovered that I have total and absolute power to step into the experience of health, wealth, love, and success at any moment I choose. That power is yours as well, if you exercise it.

Try this experiment: For one day imagine that what you have and what you are is enough. When you look in the mirror, decide to like what you see. When you connect with your friend, date, spouse, or boss, notice what you like about that person rather than what bugs you. When you go over your credit-card bill, instead of complaining about the high price of gas and groceries, thank all the people who brought your fuel to you and your food from seed to your table. When you go to work, celebrate the customers and accounts you have rather than wringing your hands over those you are missing.

If you do this experiment sincerely and continuously for even one day, your life will change. You will feel better, and things will start to work more in your favor. You will recognize that you have far more riches at your disposal than you realized. You will realize that you have not just enough, but plenty.

A Tale of Two Travelers

A traveler in an ancient time arrived at the gate of a city and found a gatekeeper sitting at its foot. "What's it like in this city?" the sojourner asked.

"What was it like where you came from?" returned the gatekeeper.

"It was a horrible place," the traveler replied. "There were no jobs, everyone was fighting with each other, and the streets were a mess."

"Well, that's pretty much what you'll find here," the gatekeeper explained.

The visitor shook his head and continued on his way.

An hour later another traveler approached the city gate. "What's it like in this city?" he asked the gatekeeper.

"What was it like where you came from?" returned the gatekeeper.

"Pretty nice, actually," the traveler replied. "My work was rewarding, people helped each other where they could, and it was a decent place for kids to grow up."

"Well, that's pretty much what you'll find here," the gatekeeper explained.

The visitor thanked the gatekeeper and entered the city.

⌒

The world you observe is not an absolute condition. It is a snapshot of your consciousness. If you want to change the world, begin by changing your vision of it. Quantum physicists tell us that it is impossible to conduct a purely objective experiment because the mere *presence* of the experimenter influences the results. Likewise, you affect your life profoundly simply by participating in it. *How* you participate determines how your life turns out.

If you are willing to shift your vision from lack to supply, you may be surprised by how much "enough" you already own. The more enough you find, the more enough you *will* find. The more lack you find, the more lack you will find. You are always finding what you are looking for, so take care what you are looking for. "Seek and ye shall find" is not a promise. It is a statement of how it already is.

My greatest teachers of enoughness were a Fijian family my beloved Dee and I were close with when we lived in that country. The mother, father, and five children, ages 2 to 15, all lived in a one-room shack with tin walls and no plumbing, electricity, or glass windows. They cooked over a wood fire, bathed in a small spring in the backyard, and walked to an outhouse in the rain. They farmed their own food and had no money for anything beyond simple necessities. From the point of view of our culture, their level of living was bare subsistence.

Oddly, these were among the happiest people I have ever met. They loved each other dearly and laughed often, and the children retained extraordinary light in their eyes even into young adulthood. The only toy the kids had was a tire swing in the backyard, and they played rugby using an empty plastic water bottle as a ball. Their shack was more of a home than many loveless mansions. They enjoyed life immensely and felt no sense of lack.

One day we bought the family a modest-size fish, perhaps 16 inches long, for their dinner. The next day I asked the dad, "Did you enjoy the fish?"

He smiled and told me, "Yes, very much! We invited the family next door for dinner. We cut up the fish, put it in a curry, and served nine people with it."

At another time we gave the father a candy bar, which he broke into pieces. "Why are you breaking it up?" I asked.

"So each of the kids can have a piece," he answered.

I cite these examples not to extol poverty, but to celebrate plenty. Sufficiency is an attitude. You might be in the midst of fabulous abundance, but not notice it because you are looking elsewhere. You might also stand in the midst of apparent devastation, but be overwhelmed by the love that moves people to join together to overcome it. Attitude is like a microscope: When you focus on dimensions deeper than the obvious, you discover vast riches that are invisible at the surface. With practice and focus, wealth becomes consistently apparent.

Wayne Dyer has enough. The kids in Fiji have enough. What do the two have in common? They would rather have enough than not enough. So they just *choose* it. Perhaps you and I could have less of what we do not want and more of what we *do* want, simply because that is what we prefer.

How do you find that sweet spot? Read on and find out.

2

IS THAT SO?

Life is God's novel. Let him write it.

— ISAAC BASHEVIS SINGER

In a small Japanese seaport town, a young woman became pregnant by a transient sailor. Not wanting the responsibility of raising the child, she named a monk in a nearby mountain monastery as the father. When the child was born, the woman's angry father took the boy to the monastery and told the monk, "My daughter has informed me that you are the father of this child. Now you must raise him."

The monk looked at the child, thought for a moment, and replied, "Is that so?" He calmly took the boy in and cared for him as if he were his own son.

Years later the mother fell ill, and on her deathbed she confessed that the child was not the monk's. Her father was appalled and returned to the monastery. He bowed to the monk and told him, "I am very sorry. My daughter has admitted her dishonesty. I will take the child back now."

The monk looked at the boy, thought for a moment, and replied, "Is that so?" Then he returned the child.

While few of us would demonstrate the monk's calm acceptance and resignation, he serves as a model of allowing what is, to be. When something challenging happens, our tendency is to try to get rid of the situation or the person who is causing it. Yet there may be greater value in gleaning the lesson the situation has come to deliver. When we extract the gift behind the appearance of trouble, the issue will dissolve not because we have pushed it away, but because we have graduated from it.

Much of our pain in life issues from resisting what comes to us, or clinging to what leaves us. Yet we have more of a choice about how much we suffer than we have been told. Pain happens, but suffering is optional.

> What comes of itself, let it come.
> What goes of itself, let it go.
> — Paramahansa Yogananda

If you believe that misery is noble, sacrifice buys you a ticket to heaven, agony pays off your karma, or dysfunction requires ongoing analysis; or if you receive pity, attention, money, or smug martyrdom for dramatizing loss, you will dwell in a world of limits and sorrow. While this reasoning seems ridiculous, many people demonstrate it by staying in situations that hurt them long after pain has delivered its message

> If you do not change direction,
> you will end up where you are heading.
> — Chinese saying

to get out of Dodge. Many people stay in abusive relationships, jobs they hate, and toxic environments even though they receive repeated messages to depart. Others cling to resentment and a sense of insult or victimization long after the incident they begrudge has come and gone. They perceive a greater reward in clinging to sorrow than in letting it go.

To keep pain from becoming suffering, minimize resistance. Decrease indignation and increase allowance. Quit trying to manipulate others, and manipulate your *viewpoint*. Find beauty, value, and purpose in what is before you. Let yourself be what you are, and let life be what it is. You might find many gifts laid at your door that you would have otherwise overlooked.

Healing Allowed

When your body is injured, it instantly sends massive healing energy to the organ that has been hurt. If you block that energy with fear or judgment or by fighting what has occurred, the healing energy hits that constriction like traffic hitting a bottleneck, and pain intensifies. If you do not tense up, but instead provide an avenue for the healing energy to flow, your pain will be minimal or even absent.

Mahatma Gandhi used the principle of nonresistance to liberate the nation of India from British rule, and more personally when he underwent an appendectomy without anesthesia. Dentists use hypnosis to help patients undergo otherwise-painful treatments and surgery. Football players severely injure a limb during a game, but keep playing for the remainder, although the injury becomes disabling afterward. You have probably had the experience of going to sleep when a part of your body hurt. While you slept, you were out of pain. When you awoke, it returned. What happened to the pain when you were asleep? The distressed organ remained in the same condition, but you removed your attention and resistance from it. Behold mind over matter: *If you don't mind, it doesn't matter.*

When I twisted my ankle while landscaping, the ankle hurt very badly and I could hardly walk. My initial thought was, *This is going to put me out of commission for a while.* Then I decided to do an experiment: I sat down and did my best to relax my ankle and allow the body's natural healing energy to take its course. After just a few moments, the ankle stopped hurting and even started to feel good. A few hours later the joint was perfect. When I allowed my body to perform its natural healing function, it was happy to cooperate. So will *your* body and other important aspects of your life realign with well-being when you allow the power within you to work on your behalf.

The Big Picture

All upset is the result of assuming that you know how life should be. You try to cram people and events into your model; and when they do not fit, you get disappointed, frustrated, and angry. But your idea of how life should be is just that—*your idea*. Usually your preconception is authored by the ego, which sees only the tiniest piece of the picture, colored by fear, and begets nonproductive results. When you fight to swim upstream while your good lives downstream, you wear yourself down and get nowhere.

I asked spiritual teacher Ram Dass, "Is it a good idea to pray for a particular result?"

He answered, "If you could be aware of all the ways that result would affect your life and the lives of everyone it touches, certainly. But no human being has the overview to know how things should turn out."

In a *Star Trek* television episode, Captain Kirk and Mr. Spock traveled back in time to the United States just before the country entered World War II. During their journey, Kirk fell in love with a famous pacifist, who had an appointment to meet with President Roosevelt in hopes of convincing him to keep the country out of the war. Meanwhile Mr. Spock found a way to research future newspaper headlines, and discovered that due to the woman's meeting with the President, the U.S. delayed entering the war, and Hitler's forces emerged victorious. Soon afterward Kirk had the chance to save the woman from a car accident, but based on Spock's prediction, he forced himself to allow the accident to occur. In so doing, he paved the way for the United States to enter the war and defeat the Nazis, who were killing millions more people than the one woman Kirk decided not to save.

While the story invites a spirited discussion of ethics and destiny, it illustrates the principle that we may not understand the effect that one action will have on the broader canvas of life. In some cases what appears to be a loss or setback may ultimately lead to results that serve the greater good. And what seems to be a gain or coup may lead to greater hardship. *A Course in Miracles* tells us,

"Some of your greatest advances you have judged as failures, and some of your deepest retreats you have evaluated as success." For this reason, we do well to practice trusting that there is a purpose to what is happening, especially the things we cannot change.

What to Pray For

My Mormon nephew volunteered at age 19 to serve on a traditional two-year mission. Caleb had never ventured very far from his Utah hometown, and the journey loomed huge and scary. Missionaries go wherever they are dispatched, live closely with another same-gender missionary they do not know, and are allowed only rare contact with home. As Caleb anticipated receiving his orders, he and his family were quite anxious about where in the world he might be sent.

I decided to pray for Caleb's proper assignment. He had said he wanted to go to Italy, so I began to pray he would be sent there. But it occurred to me that Italy might not be in the young man's best interests. Since he had grown up rather sheltered, maybe he would be more comfortable in an English-speaking nation. But then again, he would likely learn and grow more in some primitive area such as Borneo, where he would have significant adventures. My mind went round and round trying to figure out where Caleb would have the best experience.

Finally I gave up when I realized that I could not possibly know the best place for Caleb. So I simply prayed that he would be sent to a place where he would have the most rewarding personal-growth experience. The next day Caleb's mom reported that he was headed to Indianapolis, Indiana. (Go figure.)

So if it's not advisable to pray for a particular result, what *should* you pray for? Pray or intend for *qualities of experience* such as well-being, inner peace, abundance, harmony, and happiness.

Those experiences satisfy us at the deepest level and are not tied to any particular form. Our good may come to us through avenues we anticipate or through avenues we *cannot* anticipate. That's why it is useless to try to "boss" circumstances, and we should practice trust rather than anxiety-induced attempts to control.

Does saying "Is that so?" mean you should just sit around and let abuse and atrocities occur? Certainly not. If you are in a situation where someone is hurting you or someone else, or where danger or dysfunction is clear or imminent, take whatever steps are necessary to remove yourself or the other person. Trouble and addiction are not to be overlooked; they are calls for attention and correction. Acceptance is one thing; complacency is another. If you or someone close to you is clearly at risk, get out of harm's way.

Yet such situations are generally rare in relation to most choices we must make. We generally do better to give ourselves a dose of trust rather than to intensify manipulation.

If you can come to a place of release, you will experience deep peace and relief. In the words of a bumper sticker: "I gave up hope, and now I feel much better." I interpret the statement in this way: *I gave up hope that my fear-generated plan would work out, and now I feel better considering that things could work out without my fretful manipulation.*

In a society where many people are hell-bent on doing, fixing, protecting, and manipulating, the notion of allowing things to be as they are may seem preposterous. Yet there is a point at which forcing things to go as we think they should go begets diminishing returns.

Try a little less "How dare you?" and a little more "Let's see what this is all about." You might find that when you accept what's so, you end up saying, "So what?"

What could you not accept, if you but knew that everything that happens, all events, past, present and to come, are gently planned by One Whose only purpose is your good?

— *A Course in Miracles*

3

YOU ALREADY KNOW

If children grew up according to early indications,
we should have nothing but geniuses.
— JOHANN WOLFGANG VON GOETHE

Whenever I walk through a bookstore, I am amazed by all the books on the shelves for dummies and idiots. I see *Sex for Dummies, Raising Chickens for Dummies,* and *The Complete Idiot's Guide to Past Life Regression.* **Amazon.com** lists 754 books for Dummies and 200 books for Complete Idiots.

We must really think we are stupid, to need to purchase so many books for the dim-witted! I sometimes wonder if I could sell any books in a Genius series, such as *The Genius's Guide to Public Speaking,* or *Dating for Really Smart People.* Probably not. We have been so trained to think that we are brainless that when someone suggests we might be brilliant, we feel embarrassed or even argue for our incompetence.

You were not born stupid. You were born smart, with enough wisdom to navigate every passage of your life. But then you were methodically conditioned by other people who believed *they* were stupid, and passed their perceived ineptitude on to you. They taught you that you do not know, when you *do* know . . . or you have the capacity to know. My friend's son went off to his first day of kindergarten and came home crying. "The teacher told us to color in a cartoon of a clown," the boy explained. "When I colored the clown's nose green, she told me, 'That's all wrong. Everyone knows that a clown's nose is red.'" While the teacher could have congratulated the boy on his clever imagination, instead she gave him a pass to the Dummies' Club.

> I am convinced all of humanity is born with more gifts than we know. Most are born geniuses and just get de-geniused rapidly.
> — Buckminster Fuller

My friend Dr. Robert Holden, a world-renowned psychologist and expert on the science of happiness, recently welcomed his second child into his family. When I asked Robert what he had learned from being a father, he answered, "The idea that children are born as blank slates is complete bunk. Each of my children arrived with a totally unique energy and personality. Clearly they brought their own wisdom with them."

You, too, have come into this world equipped with all the wisdom you need. You just need to trust it and act on it. Contrary to what you have been told, you are not stupid. You are extremely smart. As smart as God. It's time to quit playing small and start living from your innate wisdom.

Your Internal Clock

One morning while I was walking to breakfast at a retreat center, a woman sitting beside the path asked me, "What time is it?"

I didn't have a watch, so I took a guess: "About 8:45, I believe."

The lady shook her head and replied, "No, it was 8:45 about half an hour ago."

As I walked on, I scratched my head and wondered why, if she knew that it was 8:45 half an hour ago, she needed to ask me the time. Someplace inside her, she already knew. She was just looking for confirmation.

I used to practice Orthodox Judaism, which prohibits the use of electrical devices on the Sabbath. I needed to awaken around 8 A.M. to get to the temple by 9, without using an alarm clock. So I would go to sleep on the eve of the Sabbath and set an intention to awaken at the right time. I remember several mornings on which I opened my eyes to see the second hand touching the *12* on the clock's face at precisely 8. Something inside me was perfectly aware of the time.

Something inside you, too, is perfectly aware of not just time, but timing. You know when it is time to do something and when it is time to stop. Often while I am having a conversation or a meal with someone, a moment comes when I sense that it is time to bring it to a close or leave. If I could put words to the feeling, it would say: "The purpose of this meeting is now complete, and you need to get on to your next place." When I heed that inclination, amazing synchronicities and serendipitous meetings occur, and I recognize that I am in the flow of life.

Trust your intuition and inclinations, and act on them. You are being guided at every moment.

What Would You Do If You Knew?

When I was trained as a counselor, my instructor told me, "Whenever you ask a student a question about a choice before him and he answers, 'I don't know,' ask the student, 'If you did know, what would you say?'"

I have used this technique for many years, and it works flawlessly. One day a seminar participant stated, "I want to let passion guide me, but I don't know what my passion is."

I asked the fellow, "If you did know what your passion was, what would you be doing?"

He smiled and answered, "I would ask a certain woman for a date, I would take a photography class, and I would skydive."

The audience burst into laughter and applause, since it was obvious that the fellow *did* know where his passion lived. He just *believed* he did not know, and he needed to be reminded to look within himself for his answer. You have heard that "possession is nine-tenths of the law." Well, *belief* is nine-tenths of manifesting what you want. If you believe you are stupid, you will act stupid and get stupid results. If you know you are smart, you will act smart and get smart results.

It is not arrogant to act smart. It is arrogant to act stupid, for in doing so, you are denying the genius that God has imbued you with. Claim your innate wisdom by acting as if you know, and you will find rapid and obvious confirmation.

Knowledge and Wisdom

Students in our society are rewarded lavishly for knowing trivial facts, but not for knowing how to live. Turn on any television game show and you will observe people earning washing machines, cars, and vast sums of money for remembering meaningless details and knowing the prices of material goods. Then watch elementary-school children having to pass through metal detectors to get into their classrooms, and you will understand just how inverted our value system is. We reward knowledge, but overlook wisdom. We receive money for knowing little things, but lose happiness by forgetting big things. We catalog history, but miss destiny. We know how to regurgitate data, but forget how to *live*.

Knowledge is what you learn from the outer world—facts, information, and techniques to manipulate your environment in order to survive. Wisdom is what you know from your inner world—how to connect with yourself, others, and a Higher Power; how to deliver your unique contribution; and not simply how to survive, but how to *thrive*. Knowledge helps you navigate the earth, but wisdom helps you navigate the landscape of your soul. Knowing how to get from Tucson to Los Angeles is important, but knowing how to move from fear to love is *more* important. Use your GPS when you need to, but make sure your INS (Internal Navigation System) is functioning at all times.

Many of us attended high schools or colleges that displayed the Latin phrase *Scientia potentia est* ("Knowledge is power") on the school coat of arms. Many institutions have drifted from *Scientia potentia est* to *Trivia potentia est* ("Irrelevant details are power"). I am not denying or decrying facts; I am simply suggesting that facts should advance the evolution of spirit and character, not suffocate them.

My friend Dr. Charles Mardel told me about his father, Dr. Alfred Mardel, who served as Director of Jet Propulsion for NASA during the *Apollo* space program. Dr. Mardel was one of the key individuals responsible for the extraordinary achievement of putting men on the moon. Along with being a brilliant scientist, Dr. Alfred Mardel was an astute metaphysician. He studied many sacred traditions and wrote a book on the common threads that bind esoteric pathways together.

Charles recounted that his father had a unique method of solving NASA's jet-propulsion challenges. "When my dad couldn't solve a problem in his laboratory, he would lightly hold it in mind before going to bed. Then he kept a pen and pad on his night table. Usually he received the answer during sleep, and when he awoke, he recorded his guidance. When he went back to the lab, he applied his insight to the experiment. Using this method, my father solved every NASA jet-propulsion problem within three days."

Like Dr. Mardel, you already have all the knowledge you need, or access to it. Most technical questions can be answered within seconds by doing an Internet search. Your more crucial need is to access the *Innernet*—the vast reservoir of truth embedded in your deep subconscious (or superconscious) mind.

By analogy, when a female child is born, she contains all the eggs she will pass or have fertilized during her lifetime. A woman's body does not grow new eggs. It simply draws from the resource she has owned since birth. The potential for all of her creations is already within her. Likewise, God has endowed you with a vast repository of seeds for all the good things you desire and deserve. If you are busy trying to import creations from an outside source, you may overlook the potential within you. We have been taught that the more we conquer the external universe, the more power we will gain. Yet the only power worth wielding is gained by conquering ourselves.

> How come we put a man on the moon before we figured out how to put wheels on suitcases?
> — attributed to Stephen Wright

Where to Find a Good Psychic

In my seminars I dispatch participants on an illuminating exercise. I invite folks to take a walk in pairs, during which one person has ten minutes to talk about what is most important in his or her life at the moment—events, relationships, transitions, challenges, choices, feelings . . . anything significant. The listener simply listens and does not make any comments, ask questions, or give advice. Participants generally return with compelling reports about the illumination they received. They state that they found their way to a sense of relief and empowerment about their situation, and often a solution, simply by being honest about their feelings and intentions. The answers they sought were within them.

If you are looking for a good psychic, look in the seat where you are sitting. No one knows better than you what your right path is. A psychic, coach, or counselor can help by suggesting perspectives, options, and

> A consultant is someone who borrows your watch to tell you what time it is.
> — Source unknown

possibilities to you, but those possibilities are only valid if they resonate with your inner knowing. Popular psychic Dougall Fraser wrote a book entitled *But You Knew That Already.* No truer words were ever written.

I was invited to be interviewed on a radio show for which a previously scheduled psychic guest had canceled on short notice. (One might wonder about that psychic's skills!) When the show's host began to take listeners' phone calls, many of the callers thought that *I* was the psychic. "When am I going to meet my soul mate?" one asked me. "Does my departed sister have a message for me?"

At first I explained to the callers that I was not the psychic guest they were expecting. After a while, I got tired of explaining my substitute status, and I answered the questions as if I were the psychic. "Your departed sister wants you to know that she is with you, and she loves you very much," I answered. When someone asked, "Am I on my right path?" I told her, "You certainly are."

That was true. We are always on our right path, even when it seems that we are not. And we always know, even when we think we need to ask a psychic.

Philosopher Alan Watts wrote a book entitled *The Book: On the Taboo Against Knowing Who You Are.* Perhaps *The Book: On the Taboo Against Knowing What You Already Know* would be a worthy sequel.

> No matter how often I talk to God, he never tells me anything I didn't already know.
> — Ashleigh Brilliant

In a society where most people have been trained to play dumb, it takes a courageous person to play smart.

Playing smart is far closer to the truth about you than playing dumb. Perhaps one day you or I might walk through a bookstore and see a section of books for people who know they are wise and admit it. What title would you care to contribute?

4

I Wish I Could Give You the Moon

As you sit on the hillside, or lie prone under the trees of the forest, or sprawl wet-legged on the shingly beach of a mountain stream, the great door, that does not look like a door, opens.

— STEPHEN GRAHAM

A Zen story tells of a man who came home one evening, looked through his window, and saw a thief tossing his possessions into a large sack. In Zen fashion, the home owner decided to just sit outside the door and meditate. At some point the thief saw the man and dashed out of the house. In the commotion, the home owner opened his eyes and saw that the thief had dropped a bowl from his sack.

"Wait—you forgot something!" called the home owner as he picked up the bowl and tried to catch up to the crook. But the thief was running fast and disappeared into the night.

The man stopped and took a breath. He looked up into the sky and noticed the night was illuminated by a stunning full moon. "I wish I could give you the moon," he whispered with a sigh.

⌐

This story makes no sense from a worldly point of view, since most people who discovered a thief would likely be outraged. From a higher vantage point, however, it makes perfect sense. The world as God created it is far more meaningful and valuable than any object we might possess. We already own everything worthwhile. The home owner in the story sighed because he felt compassion for the thief, who missed the magic of the moon because he was distracted by a few paltry possessions.

We all have possessions, and we want to keep them. The question is: *Do you own your possessions, or do they own you?*

If your possessions bring you joy, they are serving their purpose. If you worry about them, you have missed the moon. No one possesses the moon . . . yet everyone does. It is a gift for everyone to enjoy. If you are worried about your iPhone, car, or house, stop for a moment and look up. No one can take from you what God has given you.

A Course in Miracles tells us that the only gifts worth having are those that increase when you give them. These are the gifts of the spirit, all variations on the theme of love. When you give kindness, compassion, understanding, laughter, or forgiveness, you do not lose anything. To the contrary, both giver and receiver gain, and the blessing of the gift expands in your life and the lives of those you touch. You are bringing the eternal to Earth and nurturing it in your experience.

When you give a finite gift such as money or an object, the giver has less and the recipient has more. The *Course* would say that this is not a true gift, since in the process someone lost and someone won. The only true gifts are those that result in *everyone* winning.

When you give money or an object, the real question is: *What is the spirit that accompanies the gift?* If you are giving with a sense of guilt or obligation or you hold the receiver indebted, no gift has changed hands, because the spirit of the transaction is void. If, in contrast, you give with love, generosity, and delight, and you are happy for the recipient, the gift is real and enhances the lives of both parties.

Technology and Spirit

Over the last few centuries, we have invented phenomenal labor- and time-saving devices. But what do we *do* with the time we save? If we fill our newfound free time with more work, our technology has not freed us, but imprisoned us. More precisely, we have entrapped ourselves by becoming enamored of machines at the expense of inner peace. If we wish to find more peace, we need to choose it where we stand and not depend on machines to give it to us.

Richard Bach, the brilliant author of *Jonathan Livingston Seagull* and *Illusions,* suggests that all human inventions simply replicate faculties we already own, but which have atrophied due to disuse. Our machines represent our attempt to reclaim innate powers we have lost or forgotten.

For example, we are all inherently psychic, and anyone can communicate with anyone anywhere at any time through the invisible yet very real channel of mind. Yet most of us do not believe we possess this ability, so we invented telephones, Skype, e-mail, and texting to accomplish just that. We would like to see people far away, and know we can, so we invented television. We would like to accomplish transactions instantly without having to leave home, so we invented the Internet. Yet we can enjoy the same benefits without technology.

If you read accounts of indigenous people who do not use technology, you will find that they regularly exercise their psychic faculties, and even depend on them. (For more detailed examples, read *Mutant Message Down Under,* by Marlo Morgan; *Life and Teaching of the Masters of the Far East,* by Baird Spalding; and *Be Here Now,* by Ram Dass.)

We believe we need airplanes to travel around the globe, while many yogis (such as Sathya Sai Baba) have demonstrated bilocation. We think we need x-rays to see through things, while many intuitives accomplish this through clairvoyance. (Uri Geller was hired by an oil company to fly over fields in South America to psychically sense where oil was hidden. He was quite successful, and to this day he receives royalties for his efforts!) We have developed intricate medical technology that can detect unseen anomalies and repair them. Yet what doctors do with complicated instruments has been achieved by healers over thousands of years through subtle sensing. The traditional medicine of China and Tibet uses virtually no instruments, yet accomplishes phenomenal results.

When I see my acupuncturist, he checks my energetic pulses simply by touching my wrists for a few moments and examining my tongue. I am amazed by how accurately he can tell what's going on with my body, and how good I feel after his treatments.

Brazilian spiritual medium John of God has healed many thousands of people and performed complex surgical operations without the use of medical instruments. While this may be difficult to believe, the testimonials of patients relieved from pain and cured of diseases, many diagnosed as terminal, stand as cogent evidence that healing may be less about instruments and more about inner seeing and mobilizing the power of invisible resources.

The Technology of Prayer

Prayer is a far more effective healing technology than most people realize. Perhaps you, like me, know people who have been healed of apparently formidable or incurable conditions through the power of prayer.

My friend Carla Neff Gordan was scheduled for a second major surgery to remove several cancerous tumors. While she was in intense pain the day before she was to be operated on, Carla received a visit from Rev. Helen Thomas Irwin, who offered her a prayer in the form of a spiritual mind treatment. Irwin, a Religious Science minister, affirmed aloud that Carla was a spiritual being, created in the image and likeness of God, perfect in health and well-being. Helen concluded her treatment by telling Carla, "You are healed if you desire to be!" She then said good night and departed.

That night Carla lay in bed free of pain for the first time in a long time. While she had no previous experience with such a prayer or spiritual mind treatment, she knew one thing: she felt better. Carla began to believe that somehow the cancerous condition had been healed.

When Carla's doctor arrived the next morning to consult with her before the surgery, she asked him to please take some more x-rays prior to performing it. The annoyed doctor protested, "That won't do any good. We already have all the x-rays we need. You have advanced cancer, and we must operate immediately or you will die. Even with the surgery, you will be lucky to survive. We must operate *now!*"

Carla refused to be swayed by her physician's objections. "Unless you take more x-rays, I will refuse to have this surgery."

Exasperated, the doctor agreed and left the hospital room muttering about his ruined surgery schedule. A few hours later he returned, perplexed. "Your new x-rays came back with no sign of cancer," he told Carla. "I have no explanation, nor do my colleagues. We have studied and restudied your earlier x-rays and the new ones. I don't see any need for surgery at this point."

Carla went home and lived cancer free for the rest of her life. As a result of this healing, she went on to become an extraordinary healer herself, using spiritually based principles to transform the lives of thousands of people. (For inspiring accounts of Carla Neff Gordan's life, teaching, and ministry, visit: **www.carlaneffgordan.com**.)

Dr. Larry Dossey is one of the world's foremost authorities on the power of prayer to heal. A surgeon veteran of the Vietnam

War, Dr. Dossey has faced the most dire and grueling medical situations. Yet he has become a major proponent of prayer as a healing tool. Dr. Dossey reports that in a survey of 1,000 medical doctors, 74 percent said they believed prayer could be effective in helping heal patients. Fifty-nine percent said that they prayed for individual patients. Half of the physicians regularly prayed for their patients as a group. Fifty-five percent of the M.D.'s said they had observed miraculous recoveries in their practices. "The key to the survey was that the doctors answered anonymously," Dr. Dossey explains. "If they had to reveal their identities, they would not have admitted these experiences, since in the medical profession there is so much pressure to be scientific and not believe in spiritual faculties."

Yet spiritual faculties are just as real as medical faculties—in some ways more so. Through prayer you have direct access to the source of all healing, your doctor is available to you 24/7, and all services are free! What HMO could beat that?

I am not suggesting that you reject or bypass medical technology if you expect that it can help you. The universe has room for many successful healing modalities, and there is value in medicine and medical practices. I *am* suggesting that you use the technology of focused prayer as an adjunct to any healing course you choose—and in many cases, prayer may be a sufficient technology in and of itself.

Nature Did It First

While we tend to believe that technology improves upon nature, it more accurately replicates existing systems. The phenomenon of technology imitating nature is called *biomimicry*. Some very familiar examples of biomimicry are solar panels and Velcro. Pho-

> Good heavens, of what uncostly material is our earthly happiness composed—if we only knew it! What incomes have we not had from a flower, and how unfailing are the dividends of the seasons.
> — James Russell Lowell

tovoltaic panels capture sunlight and convert its energy to usable fuel—exactly what the cells in the leaves of green plants have been doing for three billion years!

Likewise, the idea for the popular hook-and-loop fastener Velcro came to Swiss engineer George de Mestral after he had hiked in a field with his dogs and he noticed small burs clinging to his pooches' legs. Curious, he examined how these "hitchhikers" attached tiny tendrils into the animals' fur. He went back to his laboratory and set out to replicate the tenacity of the bur. Behold the birth of the tape that secures your tennis shoes, wallet, wristwatch, iPod, and thousands of other household items.

The ideas behind solar panels and Velcro were not invented by people. They were borrowed from nature, and adapted wisely to new applications. (For a fascinating in-depth exploration of biomimicry, read *Biomimicry: Innovation Inspired by Nature*, by Janine M. Benyus.)

> Nature is just enough; but men and women must comprehend and accept her suggestions.
> — Antoinette Brown Blackwell

Ancient Simplicity and Modern Complexity

The oldest company in the world goes back 800 years. The Japanese architectural firm Tohoto specializes in building temples and pagodas. Tohoto does not use nails in their construction. Instead, they make a series of tabs on the ends of wooden pieces and fit them together. Over centuries of Japanese earthquakes, this company's structures, including five-story pagodas, have stood firm while more modern buildings around them crumbled.

Tohoto strives to build in harmony with nature, not override it. They take timber from the north-facing side of trees and install it on the north side of their pagodas, and install the wood from the south side of the trees on the south side of the pagodas. They also employ "the golden ratio," a mystical geometric proportion that occurs in nature as a relationship of parts to the whole. Mount Fuji, sacred to the Japanese, also conforms to the golden ratio, and it is used as a model for the relationship of roofs to the bodies of Tohoto's buildings.

Such craftsmanship is a vanishing art in our world of mass production. Products made by hand, with skill, intention, and care, far outshine and outlast cheaper versions that come off assembly lines. I wonder if most people's hunger for a fulfilling life is related to the relative scarcity of expertly handcrafted materials. We might satisfy that hunger by doing more things more simply, with attention to quality and detail rather than mass production with glitzy presentation for quick sale.

When I visited Egypt, I was astonished by the sophisticated structures the ancient Egyptians built. To this day scientists with technologically advanced equipment cannot explain how huge stones were lifted to build the pyramids, with such subtle engineering that a razor blade cannot slide between two stones carved to fit together! Of all the staggering achievements I observed, I was most impressed by the longevity of Egyptian paint. Craning my neck to survey the ceilings of towering temples, I learned that the original paint used to adorn the buildings was still intact. Vibrant reds, greens, and blues applied 4,000 years ago are visible today! By contrast, when I needed to paint the metal roof of my house, I went to a local superstore and purchased some paint that was guaranteed to last for ten years. Five years after its application, the paint had faded. What did the ancient Egyptians know that we have forgotten? Might we do better to return to simple quality rather than racing to produce as much as we can for the least cost?

Anthropologist Margaret Mead explained that all cultures exhibit one of three relationships to nature: (1) man *under* nature, such as the ancient Greeks and Romans, who believed their lives were controlled by gods of nature; (2) man *over* nature, such as modern Western civilization, which uses technology to overrun nature, destroying at will and taking without returning; and (3) man *in* nature, typified by most indigenous cultures, such as Native Americans, Hawaiians, Maori, and Aborigines, who respect nature, live in harmony with it, and exist in a mutually beneficial give-and-take relationship with living things.

Science lives at the tips of the branches of the tree of expanding knowledge, while spirituality lives at its roots. The environmental crises we face are wake-up calls for us to live more in accord with our deepest identity and how we fit into the universal order of creation. When we align with nature rather than fight it, it delivers immense benefits. If we receive and act on the messages before us, we will not only balance the planet, but discover our rightful place as individuals and as a civilization in the grand design of life.

The Zen of Hubble

The Hubble Space Telescope is one of the most sophisticated technological instruments ever created, enabling us to observe and study planets, stars, and galaxies in fantastic detail at unbelievable distances. The IMAX film *Hubble 3D* reveals stunning images from the edge of the known universe that are as spiritually inspirational as they are scientifically meaningful. The face of God is revealed as clearly in outer space as it is on Earth.

A crew of astronauts boarded the space shuttle *Atlantis* in May 2009 to conduct tedious repairs to the most intricate systems of the telescope. On this final mission for Hubble, the crew had many formidable tasks before them, including the delicate removal and replacement of circuit boards for an advanced camera. As astronaut Andrew Feustel hung in space reaching into the Hubble's innards, he had to remove more than 100 tiny screws that kept the sensitive equipment in place. "I have a Zen approach to doing the task," Feustel stated. "I only think about the one specific task I am doing, the one specific screw. When that screw is out, I move to the next screw. Eventually I'll get to the last one and then I'll be done. There's no point in thinking about how many screws I have ahead of me or how many I've completed. It'll just be the one screw."

I found this statement to be a poignant metaphor for the marriage of science and spirit. Here was a man working on one of the most advanced and complex machines in history, and the quiet focus of a Zen master enabled him to achieve his goal. There is no argument between science and spirit, except in minds that do not grasp the magnitude of both. At some point

> The true man walks the earth as the stars walk the heavens, grandly obedient to those laws which are implanted in his nature.
> — Lemuel K. Washburn

the simple and the advanced meet and merge to enable a grander experience than either can offer without the other.

Like the Zen home owner who wished he could give the thief the moon, we might do well to look up and recognize that we already own what we are striving for. Images captured by the Hubble telescope from distant galaxies look astonishingly like ones we know on Earth: eyes, butterflies, and sperm fertilizing an egg. Could it be that all the gifts creation has to offer exist under our feet as well as over our heads? Might the answer to our environmental crises be within us? It may be simplistic, even radical, to find satisfaction in the world as God created it, but ultimately that may be the very awareness that saves us.

Some day, after we have mastered the wind, the waves, the tides, and gravity, we shall harness for God the energies of love. Then, for the second time in the history of the world, we will have discovered fire.

— **Pierre Teilhard de Chardin**

5

DON'T JUST
DO SOMETHING

A truly good man does nothing,
Yet leaves nothing undone.
A foolish man is always doing,
Yet much remains to be done.

— LAO-TSU, THE TAO TE CHING
(TRANSLATED BY GIA-FU FENG AND JANE ENGLISH)

Most self-help books give you lists of things to do: **10 Steps to Unclutter Your House . . . 20 Surefire Exercises to Get Washboard Abs . . . 30 Ways to Keep Your Man from Straying.** These books and methods can be quite helpful if you get your house tidied, trim your tummy, and hold on to your man.

Yet most self-help books do not tell you how to cultivate a sense of inner peace that will permeate and improve all aspects of your life. They tell you what to do, but not how to *be*. If you can master the art of being, effective doing flows naturally. Some of my coaching

> If something you're doing isn't working,
> doing more of it will not work any better.
> — Source unknown

clients are type A "do"-aholics. They are on a constant rampage of doing, seeking to achieve more, more, more. "Tell me what to do!" they demand in coaching. Yet for them the answer is not more doing. They already know how to "do." What they need to learn is how to *be*.

My friend Kit's life is a series of constant errands, dramas, and emergencies. She cannot sit still for more than a few minutes before she has to get up and do something or go somewhere. As I got to know Kit, I wondered what was behind her obsessive doingness. Then one day she revealed that she had been raised in a religion that taught her to feel guilty about everything. If anything goes wrong in Kit's world or the world of anyone around her, she assumes it is her fault. On some level, Kit believes she is damaged or even evil, which is ludicrous, since she is a kind, responsible, and generous person. She just does not know it. So she is afraid to face herself. Kit believes that if she were to look upon her true self, she would see someone so hideous that she would run out of the room screaming. Nothing could be further from the truth.

But belief is powerful, so Kit's belief in guilt rules her life. She creates an endless array of fires to put out so she will not have to face her painful feelings about herself. The irony is that if Kit sat down and really looked herself in the eye, she would find a beautiful person. But the prerequisite for such a profound encounter would be to stop "doing" for even a little while.

Doing is effective when it is inspired by joy and purpose. When doing is motivated by fear, guilt, avoidance of feeling, or the need to prove oneself, no real movement accrues, except a return to the crossroads of love and fear, where the sojourner can make a new choice based on wholeness.

When to Act

If you have a decision or problem before you, you may feel that you need to do *something*—because the simple act of doing something makes you feel like you are moving toward a solution.

Yet real solutions issue only from a shift in consciousness. Einstein is said to have declared, "Problems cannot be solved by the same level of thinking that created them." *A Course in Miracles* echoes, "You cannot be your guide to miracles, for it was you who made them necessary."

Instead of reacting impulsively to your problem, look at it from different angles, sleep on it, pray or meditate about it, consult with people you trust and respect, take a breather, and do something that takes your mind off of it. Then, when you feel refreshed or inspired, ap-

> Don't just do something. Stand there.
> — attributed to Buddha

proach your challenge or decision from a more expanded perspective. Most likely you will see options and solutions you could not see when you were upset or confused. Confusion is not your natural state, although you may have become so accustomed to it that it feels normal. Clarity is natural, and cultivating a peaceful demeanor will give you the space to know precisely what to do, when you need to do it.

The Power of Being

Western culture is hell-bent on doing. We get things done, but lose our soul in the process. Other cultures are more established in *being*. They live in the moment; savor the simple things in life; and value their connection with family, friends, and community. If you would like to master the art of being, study or spend some time with people in South Seas cultures such as Hawaii, Bali, or Fiji, or with any equatorial culture. You are more likely to find natives relaxing than working late. You or I might criticize them for being lazy

> Besides the noble art of getting things done, there is the art of leaving things undone. The wisdom of life consists in the elimination of non-essentials.
> — Lin Yutang

or nonproductive, yet they *find* happiness in ways that many people in our culture *long* for it. Your first impression may be that such people seem primitive or ignorant, but as you get to know them, you will discover extraordinary spiritual wisdom. They may not have iPods, but they have *iAm.*

Let's turn again to a *Star Trek* episode for a metaphysical lesson. When a Klingon warship arrived at peaceful Organia to pillage the planet for its ore resources, the *Enterprise* captain urged the Organians to defend themselves. But they refused, stating that they had no interest in war. The *Enterprise* crew could not stand to see these innocent people suffer this plundering, so they prepared to fight the Klingons on the Organians' behalf. As the battle was about to begin, the instrument panels of both ships became too hot to manipulate. Then both warring factions discovered that the Organians were not really primitive, but extremely advanced; they had grown beyond war and would not have it in their midst. So they psychically disabled the fighters' weapons. The Organians then revealed themselves as beings of pure energy who used the planet simply for recreation.

We do not need to warp to Organia to behold models of power leveraged by consciousness. Martial artists and yoga masters have been manifesting maximal results with minimal effort for thousands of years. I saw a video of a Qigong master in China who invited half a dozen strong men to push him over. Although they tried with all their might, they could not do it. Then the master was able to knock each of these men to

> Give me a place to stand and with a lever I will move the whole world.
> — Archimedes

the ground with a touch of his finger. His power was established in the inner stillness he had gained through a lifetime of practice.

Our culture has more to gain from inner stillness than incessant pushing. When a quiet mind generates action, it is far more effective than one that is scattered or running on a psychic treadmill. If you know how to *do,* without knowing how to *be,* you have not learned life's most poignant lesson. Merge action with inner clarity and you become the master of life.

Words and Silence

Words express doing, while silence expresses being. Silence can be a more powerful form of communication than words. If you need to fill space with words, you miss the gift of silence.

Dutch psychologist Namkje Koudenburg found that people in conversation become uncomfortable after four seconds of silence. That is not a very long time. We have been conditioned through a barrage of rapid-fire sound bites in television, radio, movies, and the Internet to keep words and music streaming at lightning speed. Consequently, when we are confronted with silence, we feel disoriented and insecure.

A friend of mine organized a campaign in her school system to encourage families to spend an occasional evening without television. To her surprise, she received a great deal of resistance— not from the students, but from the parents. The kids thought it would be fun, but the parents freaked out because they feared they would lose their electronic babysitters and actually have to interact with their kids. Good God, anything but *that!*

Consider, by contrast, the tradition of the Quakers, who in their prayer meetings invite members to sit in silence and listen for the voice of God. When a member is so inspired to speak that he is *quaking,* then he may do so. That is how the name "Quaker" was born.

I know a fellow who leads an annual retreat in Assisi, Italy, the home of St. Francis. The retreat is basically silent. The rule is: "Speak only if what you have to say is more powerful than the silence." Imagine how commanding our communication would be if we practiced this principle on a daily basis!

If you do not know what to say, say nothing. Do not talk just to fill space. You might find that you truly enjoy being with friends or family in a quiet way. In the rural area where I live, electrical power occasionally goes out for a few minutes or

> Just be quiet and still and the world will offer itself to you to be unmasked . . .
> It will roll in ecstasy at your feet.
> — Franz Kafka

hours. When the power fails in the evening, Dee and I light candles and oil lamps, and we nestle on the couch with each other and our dogs. No TV, videos, computers, radio, music, or electronic stimulation of any kind. We love it! We always say, "Let's not wait for the power to go out to do this. Let's do this by choice more often." And we do.

You, too, might like to give yourself an occasional evening without electronic stimulation. You might be amazed by how the quiet clears your head and soothes your soul.

Willing to Wait

Patience is a virtue many of us could benefit from developing. I am not a good "waiter." I want it all, and I want it now. Once I cut to the front of a long line at an airport. I did not mean to. Afterward Dee asked me, "Did you see that line of people you stepped in

> And let patience have its perfect work, that ye may be perfect and entire, lacking in nothing.
> — James 1:4

front of?" Actually, I didn't. In a way, it is valuable to be so focused that you expect rapid manifestation and do not notice obstacles. At the same time, it's wise to be present with what is happening and harmonize with the people around you. You would not want to fast-forward through a good movie. That's why there is a PLAY button.

Impatience is not a time issue or a mark of selfishness. It is a trust issue and a statement of fear. *A Course in Miracles* tells us, "Patience is natural to those who trust." Things happen when they are ripe—not before or after. If you try to force something before it is ready, it won't work. If you wait too long, it won't work either. If you watch for signs and openings, you will recognize when it is time to act.

If you are striving to make something happen and your efforts

> If you can't pray a door open, don't try to pry it open.
> — Source unknown

are not being rewarded, you may be trying to push the river. Sometimes the river flows rapidly, and sometimes it lolls along more

34

slowly. A good boat captain works with the current, not against it. The river will take you where you want to go if you let it be your friend.

Don't try to make anything happen. *Let* it happen. Attempts to force indicate that you are immersed in a "struggle" mentality, the least optimal orientation for success. Great things happen *through* you. The more you cooperate with the spirit of greatness and ignore the promptings of fear, the more effective you will be and the fewer black-and-blue marks you will sport.

> The greatest power uses the lightest touch.
> — Bashar

The Master's Formula

If you have read self-help books or participated in seminars that teach the power of the mind, you have been taught that you can create what you desire by visualizing. Yet visualization comes to life through the medium of action. No matter how much you have visualized, at some point you need to get up and do something.

I worked with a fellow who was promoting a seminar for me. When he wasn't making much progress attracting clients, he told me, "Maybe it's time to go back and do some more dreaming." But all he had done was dream. He needed to follow up on visioning with action.

Spiritual principles and techniques work, but they can turn into excuses or sidetracks. It is important to charge your car's battery, but if you never drive it because you are always charging it, you get no value out of your car.

Here is a powerful formula for manifestation:

1. Conceive.
2. Believe.
3. Visualize.
4. Act.
5. Release.

Step 4, action, is a crucial element. Do everything you can to make your dream come true, without anxiety or fear. Then allow

> Pray as if it all depends on God.
> Act as if it all depends on you.
> — Source unknown

God to do God's part. When you have acted with responsibility and integrity and done everything you know how to do, let go and allow the universe to orchestrate the details.

Develop your power to step back and just be. From the sanctuary of quietude, you will know what needs to be done. When you feel filled, whole, clear, energized, and enthusiastic, march on to the high calling of your spirit.

One of my coaching clients was torn between getting back together with her former boyfriend or going out with new acquaintances. I told her that before she could do either, she had to process her recent breakup and get clear on who she was and what she wanted. "You have to go in before you can go out," I told her.

Many circumstances call for action, but *all* call for clarity. Cultivate the quality of being, and doing will proceed with ease, grace, dignity, and success that represents your unique touch empowered by a greater hand.

Sitting quietly, doing nothing, spring comes and the grass grows.

— ZEN PROVERB

6

GOING NOWHERE FASTER

There is more to life than increasing its speed.

— ATTRIBUTED TO **MAHATMA GANDHI**

Sometimes I feel like we are all living in the movie *Speed*, trapped on a bus that cannot slow down. The pace of our lives just keeps going faster and faster until we have to struggle with all our might just to keep up.

The computer you just ordered is obsolete by the time it reaches your door, speed-dating gives you one minute to decide if you like someone, you can get married in Las Vegas without the awful inconvenience of having to step out of your car, books that you once had to go to a store to buy show up on your Kindle screen with one click, and the Chinese just deployed a train that hurtles at 302 miles per hour. Meanwhile the earth is spinning at 1,000 miles per hour, orbiting the sun at 67,000 miles per hour. Stillness, it turns out, is pure illusion!

You would think that increasing the *speed* of life would increase the *quality* of life. Yet it is not so. When 1957 pollsters asked a population, "Are you happy?" about 60 percent of respondents reported that they were happy. When a recent poll posed the same question, about 57 percent said they were happy. We are going everywhere much faster, except toward happiness.

The speed at which you act is a function of the distance you perceive between where you are and where you want to be. The more you believe that "there" is better than "here," the more you hurry to close the gap.

> Slow down and everything you are chasing will come around and catch you.
> — attributed to John De Paola

Yet if you eased up on the throttle, you might find that what you are rushing to get to is already here. Then you won't have to hurry to get there. I sometimes fantasize about producing a bumper sticker: GOING NOWHERE FASTER WON'T GET YOU SOMEWHERE.

The ability to move faster does help. Given the choice between driving from New York to Los Angeles in five days and flying there in five hours, I usually take the plane. Yet as I gaze down onto the Grand Canyon from 35,000 feet, I recall cherished road trips on which I sat for a whole day with my feet dangling over the edge of the great abyss, staring with utter awe into a gap that mules could fathom, but not my mind. Those cross-country trips took longer, but showed me endless fields of sunflowers, introduced me to fascinating back-country people I never would have met on an airplane, and gave me a reprieve from jet lag. If you've never done it, try driving across America. Road trek can be just as wondrous as *Star Trek*.

I live near the world-famous Hana Highway, one of the most scenic drives in the world. This spectacular Maui road winds through lush rain forests, pierces the hem of stunning waterfalls, and overlooks steep drop-offs with breathtaking vistas of rugged lava-rock shorelines. The 30-mile ribbon measures but two thin lanes wide (sometimes less), traversing an astounding 620 curves and 54 one-lane bridges. The reward for staying with the drive—thrilling for some and challenging for others—is a snapshot of paradise most people remember for a lifetime.

If you were to ride the Hana Highway all the way to the tiny town after which it is named, you might be surprised to find but a sleepy village with a couple of grocery stores, a gas station, and an understated hotel. Upon arrival, some tourists throw their hands up and grunt, "I made that whole nerve-racking trip for *this?*" They do not realize that the purpose of the trip is not to get to Hana. The purpose of the trip is the ride.

Two types of drivers cruise the Hana Highway: those who are busy getting there, and those who are busy being there. The average speed possible, due to the narrowness of the road and the one-lane bridges, is 20 miles per hour. You can't go much faster even if you try. The Hana Highway is in itself a meditation and a message: The slower you go, the more you see. Some rides are meant to get you places. Some rides *are* the places.

Metaphorically speaking, rides that oblige you to slow down are an invitation to enjoy a view you might otherwise overlook. People who lose their jobs or are forced by illness to stay home or in bed, parents of children with disabilities, and airline travelers facing a delay often report that their challenge is but a veiled blessing or lesson. They are forced to be present where they are, an experience they did not know they were missing. Some people report that their setback was the best thing that ever happened to them. The setback was actually a *setup.*

Living at the Speed of Choice

If you think you have to go fast all the time and don't realize that slower is an option, you don't have a choice. But you *do.* You can choose to find enough *here* rather than when you get *there.* Or with your present partner instead of your fantasy lover. Or with this job instead of that one. Or with the house you own instead of the one you want. I'm not saying you have to stay with your partner, job, or house. I'm just saying that you *can.*

Sometimes the willingness to find your good where you stand is the prerequisite to moving to "better." As long as you need to go, you have to stay. When you can stay, you are free to go. It's a paradox—your point of power. As long as you are attached to one option or the other, you are stuck. When you can hold both alternatives simultaneously, you are free.

Sometimes I have a hard time getting away from my computer. It is what some people would call a "soft addiction." There always seems to be just one more e-mail to answer, another Facebook friend request to confirm, another recommended YouTube video to watch, a final sentence I need to polish on my article. Some little devil crouching behind the screen is grabbing me by the neck, shouting, *"Don't leave now! You're not done yet!"*

In a *Twilight Zone* episode, a distraught fellow could not tear himself away from a slot machine. Wherever he turned, there was the machine, egging him on to feed it just one more quarter. Perhaps the personal computer is a new incarnation of that slot machine. You put lots of coins in, and once in a while you get a few out. Is it really worth it?

Sometimes Dee finds me sitting at the computer long after I said I would join the family. "Step away from the computer, sir," she commands in the gravelly voice of a Highway Patrol officer. At that point I know she's right, and I admit it, which pleases her to no end.

There are two ways to get what you want: (1) you can manipulate your environment, or (2) you can manipulate your attitude. Sometimes you can manipulate your environment. *Always* you can manipulate your mind. If you can't rearrange your external furniture, then find a way to come to peace with where you are or what you have to do. Contentment does not depend on stuff, but ideas. Stuff is outside you; ideas are inside you. Other people might control the world around you, but only *you* control the world within you. Ultimately ideas are more powerful than people, things, or events. So regardless of what the news tells you, you really do have power over your life.

The most self-defeating thing you can do is to take action with divided intentions. If you are doing something while resisting, resenting, or complaining about it, you are ripping yourself off, along with everyone else involved. Nothing is more annoying than someone doing something and kvetching and whining as they do it. Either do something with a whole heart or don't do it. If you agree to do something, then really do it. If you don't agree to do it, then really don't do it. *Be total.*

I'm probably not going to slow down the world by suggesting that we all take it a little easier, breathe a little more as we go, and consider whether running "there" is really better than enjoying "here." But I can make *my* world more peaceful and happier by taking my time, and so can you. You are not in charge of the world, but you are in charge of *your* world.

A friend of mine is a lawyer in a large, successful firm. When she redecorated her office with a mauve color scheme, a feng shui fountain, and an aromatherapy diffuser, her colleagues made fun of her. But then they started to come to her office to hang out. "It feels really nice in here," they would comment, and then stay until she had to ask them to leave because she had work to do!

You may not be the boss of the firm, but you are the boss of your space and your experience. You have the right and power to move at a pace that feels good and works for you, no matter what pace others move at, or what they would choose for you. In the end all choice lies in your domain, and until you exercise it, you will feel disempowered. Choose consciously, and the power you have diverted to the outer world will return to you. Then, at peace with yourself and your choices, you will inspire others to make choices that nourish them.

Ultimately there is nowhere to get to. If you could fully be here, you would not need to get there. But—back to the paradox—the more you can be here, the more you can get there. Going nowhere faster won't get you somewhere. Fully embracing *here* might reveal to you that you have already arrived at the *there* you were rushing toward.

7

Happy to Ride in Cargo

Happiness is not a destination. It is a method of life.

— ATTRIBUTED TO **BURTON HILLS**

As Dee and I took our bulkhead seats on a flight home to Hawaii, we noticed a young couple seeking their seats across the aisle from us. They were on their honeymoon, very much in love, and excited about their adventure. When they realized they were assigned to sit apart from each other—in middle seats, one row behind the other—both of their countenances dropped like a couple of five-year-old kids whose ice-cream cones had fallen on the sidewalk.

The passenger seated next to the husband, a woman probably the age of the bride's mother, sensed their distress and kindly offered to switch seats with the bride so she could sit next to her husband. The young lady was delighted, and the women changed places. As the kind woman took her new seat, I complimented her, "That was very generous of you to trade your bulkhead aisle seat for a middle one farther back."

The lady smiled and answered, "I was a newlywed once, and I know how she feels. Besides, I'm going to Hawaii! I would ride in the cargo compartment if I had to!"

Her comment caught me by surprise. Dee and I travel a great deal, and we are fussy about where we sit; we make extensive efforts to get roomy seats on airplanes. This woman, by contrast, was in such a state of joy and appreciation that she was delighted to simply be on the plane. Her exhilaration was so great that she created a miracle for the newlyweds. She demonstrated that happiness is more about attitude than conditions. When you find contentment within yourself, it spills over onto others and may even create miracles.

As the plane hurtled skyward, I began to reconsider my fussiness. My happiness was conditional upon getting my chosen seat. That woman's happiness was *un*conditional because she chose it. Even though the plane we were both riding on leveled off at 35,000 feet, she was flying closer to heaven.

<hr />

We all want to get what we want, and we try to do what it takes to get our choices.

The question is: Can you still be happy if you don't get your first choice? Have you grown so used to having what you want that you have forgotten your appreciation for getting it the first time? Do you take your good for granted, or are you grateful for it every time you receive it?

In Shunryu Suzuki's classic book *Zen Mind, Beginner's Mind*, he underscores the importance of approaching every experience with a clean slate, like the mind of a child. If we become jaded and our threshold of need becomes too high, we miss the joy of our journey and the wide-eyed delight in what is right before us.

Joseph Campbell issued the now-famous advice "Follow your bliss." One objection I sometimes hear to this maxim is: "But if everyone followed their bliss, we'd have a world of selfish people competing for their personal bliss and hurting each other in the process." The answer is that true bliss runs deeper than immediate gratification. To some people, bliss simply equates with sensual delight such as playing *Twister* naked, with a group of friends drenched in Mazola oil. While that might be fun, a more mature level of bliss might derive from doing something that would make another person happy. To thrill your skin is one thing; to fulfill your soul is another. The act of kindness on the airplane created bliss on two levels: the newlyweds got to sit together, while the other passenger enjoyed the pleasure of seeing them happy.

Happy people do not demand a lot from the world, because their happiness proceeds from a place deeper than the world can touch. They regard life as a gift and celebrate what comes to them. Such simple pleasures do not result in self-abnegation, but serve as a magnet by which the Law of Attraction heaps more treasures at their feet.

> There are so many men who can figure costs, and so few who can measure values.
> — Source unknown

There are two ways to ride first class: one is in the front of the plane, and the other is at the bottom of your heart.

8

NO DRAMAS, MATE

To see your drama clearly is to be liberated from it.

— KEN KEYES, JR.

In America we use several phrases to let other people off the hook. "No problem," "No worries," and "No sweat" are welcome answers to a request for help, or a potential dilemma. When I visited Australia, I learned another phrase that is even more liberating. When my hostess got lost driving me to an event and I realized we would be late, I phoned the program sponsor and apologized to him.

"We'll see you when we see you," he told me. "No dramas, mate."

No dramas. Now there's an affirmation. While many of us accept drama as a fact of life, or even a *way* of life, we might do well to question if drama is really necessary. Can you live without it?

The experience of drama is built on multiple illusions:

— First, there are good guys and bad guys. This is entirely subjective, since even the meanest antagonist sees himself as the protagonist. One hidden payoff for being involved in a drama is that you reinforce your desired identity by disparity: if you think you are a good guy or want to be one, you need a bad guy to show, by contrast, that you are right or heroic.

— Next, the good and bad guys duke it out to see who will win. In the *Mad* magazine cartoon series *Spy vs. Spy,* two spies, one wearing white and the other black, are eternally trying to trick each other to gain the advantage or do away with the foe. No one ever wins.

— Next, drama assumes a victim position on the part of the protagonist. Someone stronger is trying to hurt someone weaker, and the underdog has to struggle to overcome the greater evil. Behold the theme of practically every novel, stage play, and motion picture ever produced.

Yet unlike the book, play, or movie in which the little guy usually triumphs and you close the novel or walk out of the theater satisfied with a happy ending, in real life the victim position is self-reinforcing and perpetuates itself. The more you see yourself as a victim, the more people and things victimize you. You might experience momentary triumphs, but just around the corner lurks the next evil. Not because that's reality or destiny, but because you keep seeing yourself as powerless, you affirm your predicament in thought and word, and you continue to attract situations that prove your expectation. When you realize that you are in charge of your own life and no one can take your good from you unless *you* give it to them, the story changes. Victimhood ends when you cease to see through the lens of victim consciousness.

— Finally, a drama contains doubt or tension about the outcome. Will the big bad guys win, or can the little guy overcome? *A Course in Miracles* tells us that the word *challenge* is meaningless, for it implies doubt about the outcome. The *Course* assures us that everything ultimately works out.

Challenges are formidable only to the small self. The higher self—the real you—is greater than any situation it encounters. So while the contracted version of you says, "Oh no!" the expanded version says, "Ah, interesting!" Broader awareness transforms frustration into fascination and finds pathways to a positive outcome.

Drama can also be an addiction. Many people grow accustomed to a certain amount of ongoing turmoil, and they gravitate to a set point for drama in their lives. If their drama level falls below a certain threshold, they find some new source of mayhem to bring their adrenaline back up to speed. By contrast, people with few dramas know how to cut back on this element if it exceeds their comfort level. People

> Just because you shine in a crisis doesn't mean you need a crisis to shine.
> — Abraham-Hicks

who have lots of drama in their lives always have lots of drama, people who have a moderate amount of drama always have a moderate amount of drama, and people who have little or no drama always have little or no drama. This consistency is not based on luck or stars; it is based on consciousness and choice.

The good news is that even if you have *had* lots of drama, you are free to make a new choice and lower your threshold if you wish. Some people get sick of drama (sometimes literally), and they decide to shift their awareness and intention so that these circumstances diminish or disappear. A movie reviewer described a film character as "the kind of guy who doesn't have any problems because he doesn't want any." That option is equally available to you and me.

The first step to activate this shift is to notice when dramas arise and be conscious about how you respond to them. Most people are so immersed in their drama that they are unwilling to own their part in creating it. When I gently suggested to one of my clients that she seemed to have lots of dramas going on around her, she became quite defensive and even insulted. In light of her response, I chose not to challenge or argue with her; she was not ready to face her role as generator of her experiences. She would have to come to that realization in her own way and timing.

If you are ready to end a drama pattern, here's how to do it: When you find yourself becoming enmeshed in such a situation, take a deep breath; step back for a moment; center yourself as well as you can; and ask yourself, "How would I deal with this if it were not a big drama? What if this was all just data or information, and a resolution did not require upset?" From that position you may see options you would not recognize if you were otherwise embroiled. If there is an action you need to take, take it—but do so from a sense of confidence, ease, and trust rather than ire or desperation. Perhaps you do not even need to *do* anything. Most actions that people take when faced with a perceived drama spring from reaction, protection, or retaliation—all motivations that rarely obtain worthwhile results. Unless you are sure you have to do something, and can do it with a sense of calm assurance, try doing nothing. You may be surprised by how things work themselves out in the absence of frantic attempts to control. If you need to do something, you will be guided as to what, when, and how. Otherwise wait until you know.

> Always take an emergency leisurely.
> — Norman Vincent Peale

I do not mean to dismiss or demean difficulties that may arise. We all have situations that test our inner peace. I am simply suggesting that we may find more of that peace by questioning the need for drama and rising above it rather than succumbing to the tumult it engenders.

All circumstances and events are invitations to remember the pervasive nature of well-being, no matter what appearances indicate. You have access to a Higher Power that can help you in ways you cannot help yourself. The success of 12-step recovery methods is based on the tenets "My life became unmanageable" and "We made a decision to turn our will and our lives over to the care of God."

Drama is one of the ways your life may feel unmanageable. (Would we do well to add "Drama Anonymous" to the roster of

12-step programs?) The form of your issue or addiction is less important than the power that overcomes it. That power lives within you, surrounds you, and energizes you when you need it. But you must be open to asking for help and receiving it.

I received a fax from Louise L. Hay, who dispatched this memo to all of the authors associated with Hay House publishing. In huge bold letters the fax read:

> DEAR ALAN,
> I WILL BE HANDLING ALL OF YOUR PROBLEMS TODAY,
> SO I WON'T NEED ANY HELP FROM YOU.
> HAVE A GREAT DAY.
> YOURS TRULY, GOD.

While the memo was tongue-in-cheek, the message was spot-on: You have a source of wisdom and strength that can entirely undo the stress of a drama or multiple dramas if you let it. You can and will grow beyond drama when you realize that what it offers cannot satisfy you. Your spirit runs stronger and deeper than any part of your personality immersed in drama, and when you proceed from your greater self, you can say with full authority, like my enlightened Australian sponsor, "No dramas, mate."

9

SEEKERS AND
FINDERS

*A man travels the world over in search of what
he needs and returns home to find it.*

— GEORGE MOORE

"Why have you never gotten married?" Jamil asked his friend the Sufi rascal-sage Nasrudin.

Nasrudin sighed. "All of the significant women in my life have had tragic flaws."

"Like what?"

"First there was Samantha, from London. She was very sweet, but her nose was quite large. I couldn't overlook it. Olga the Russian heiress was gorgeous, but a dull lover. Then there was Stella, an Italian. She was passionate, but emotionally volatile."

"Have you ever met a woman you thought you could be with?" Jamil asked.

"Ah, yes," Nasrudin answered. "Ingrid from Sweden was perfect in every way. She was stunningly attractive, intelligent, good-natured, and an awesome lover—my dream woman down to every detail."

"Then why didn't you marry her?" Jamil had to ask.

"She was looking for a perfect man."

We all have our vision of our ideal mate, job, home, or life-style. Some of us have made long "laundry lists" of our desired partner or situation down to minute details.

Such a list can be a very useful exercise to help you identify your intentions for, let's say, a relationship. When someone actually shows up, however, you may find that your partner does not precisely match your ideal: he leaves his clothes on the floor; she nags; you are a spender, while your partner is a saver; she can't say no to her parents; he has baggage with his former wife. Perhaps flaws run deeper, such as an addiction or debt habit. Contrary to your vision, you find yourself with a human being with both attractive qualities and characteristics that annoy the hell out of you.

At such a point you have to decide if you will keep looking for "the one" or let the current one be "the one." If your relationship is beset with problems, you may do better to move on. But in many cases you may be able to find what you are looking for where you are. Your task may not be to replace your relationship, but to shift your vision. If you change your situation without changing your mind, you are headed for a repeat. Upgrade your viewpoint and you optimize satisfaction.

If you leave your current partner in quest of someone better, you might find someone else without your original partner's flaws. But after the initial thrill, you will likely discover that your new partner also has flaws—just different ones. Partner number one had seven out of ten characteristics you value, and partner number two also has seven out of ten—just a different seven out of ten. Ten out of ten is a noble ideal, but a rare result. Is the "switching cost" really worth it?

You can tell what you are looking for by what you are finding. If your intention is to be satisfied, you will notice things that satisfy you. If you perceive a payoff in noticing what is dissatisfying, you will find more and more to be dissatisfied about. At every moment you are inventing and reinventing your partner, job, home, and life. You do not see your partner as he or she is. You see *your idea* of who your partner is.

My friends Jerry Jampolsky and his wife, Diane Cirincione, have enjoyed a loving marriage for many years. Diane told me, "I used to get irritated when Jerry would make toast in the morning and leave a trail of bread crumbs on the kitchen counter. I asked him to clean up after his ritual, but he kept forgetting. Every morning I would walk into the kitchen, find the crumbs, and feel irritated.

"Then one day it occurred to me that the only thing worse than finding the trail of crumbs would be to walk into the kitchen and not find the crumbs because Jerry wasn't there. At that moment I began to see the crumbs as a symbol of his presence, and I appreciate him even more."

You can focus on the trail of crumbs or on how much you love your partner, and you will get more of whatever you focus on. Which do you value more?

Love at a Distance

Sometimes what appears to be the search for perfection is actually a search for *imperfection*. Finding flaws in potential partners can be a way of keeping love at a distance. If you fear intimacy or any other aspect of a close relationship, you may turn minor issues into deal breakers and thus ensure the freedom, control, or any other benefit you perceive in your singledom that you fear you might lose in a relationship.

In the film *Shallow Hal*, a fellow named Mauricio keeps finding things wrong with the women he dates. At one point he dumps a fabulous woman. When the main character, Hal, asks Mauricio why he broke up with the lady, he explains that her second toe was too long and he could not stand looking at it.

While Mauricio's explanation sounds ridiculous, it is not much more outlandish than some of the reasons some of us have cited for turning our backs on potential partners or successful situations. We fixate on one undesirable aspect until that looms in our minds as someone's entire identity. Meanwhile we could focus on more desirable aspects as his or her true identity, and be uplifted and empowered by that. Perception is a choice.

When I was dating various women and not finding one I wanted to be with, a friend showed me a cartoon of a skeleton sitting on a park bench. The caption said: "Waiting for Mr. Right." The cartoon got my attention, for I realized that if I did not become less choosy, I might end up like the skeleton!

Not long afterward I began to date Dee, and I enjoyed her company a great deal. At first I had fears and concerns about our relationship, and I was tempted to keep her at arm's length. But something inside urged me to give her and our relationship a chance. When I did, I found that my concerns were extremely minor compared to all the fulfilling elements of our connection. Now I'm really glad that I let Dee's magnificence be her reality, for our relationship is a blessing I cherish more each day.

Seek and Find

A Course in Miracles tells us that the ego's motto is "Seek and do not find." The motto of the higher self is "Seek and find," or simply, "Find." Seeking is fine as long as you are *willing* to find. Some people are so immersed in the process of seeking or in their identity as a seeker that they would be lost and disoriented if they found what they sought. In the classic film *The Princess Bride,* Inigo Montoya dedicates his life to finding the man who assassinated his father and avenging the crime. Finally Inigo tracks down the assassin and does him in. Afterward he stops in his tracks as a stunned look washes over his face. He confesses that he has been in that revenge business so long that now he does not know what to do with his life.

Many people have been in the "seeking" business for so long that they do not know what they would do if they "found." They develop identities, belief systems, causes, relationships, and support systems based on the idea *I don't have what I want and need, and I am trying to (or can't) get it.* They do not consider that they might already have what they need, or that they might be able to get it with far less angst and effort than they have been expending.

No one does anything unless he believes that what he will get in return is equal or greater in value than what he is giving in order to get it. People who constantly seek without finding perceive greater reward in seeking than they do in finding. They may romanticize their identity as a seeker, get attention or pity for their problem, receive money for their pain, be supported by government or family subsidies, feel satisfaction in being "right," gain fellowship and reinforcement from others who have the same problem, or feel safe in their familiar situation and insecure if it were to change. When confronted with the possibility of fulfilling their quest or solving their problem, they sense that their known world might be rocked, so they choose to stay with their crusade rather than let it end.

Such people do not realize that their *perceived* reward in continuing to seek is just that—perceived. If they recognized that seeking is costing them more than they are gaining, they would choose to *find*. The cost of seeking is to maintain an identity of being small, empty, powerless, victim-

> Give up your lust for growth.
> — White Eagle

ized, or absent of love. The reward for finding is to claim your power to choose *all* of your life, including health, wealth, love, and inner peace. Put like this, the equation is a no-brainer.

Take some time to consider if you have developed an identity or lifestyle as a seeker or someone with a particular problem. What rewards might you be gaining from clinging to your sense of lack or your quest? What are the costs? Then consider what the rewards might be if you were willing to heal your issue or complete your quest. In doing so, you will tip the scales in favor of finding, and graduate from seeking.

Greetings, Pilgrim

A popular television commercial depicted a group of people, each holding a candle, wandering through a dark room. After a while a light came on, and the announcer proclaimed, "Greetings, pilgrim. Your search is ended!" Then they found a can of coffee of the brand the commercial was advertising.

The commercial was on to a universal principle. It may be time to say "Enough already" to your identity as a seeker. Seeking is fine if it's fun and your quest leads to a positive result. But if you just keep going in circles or coming up empty-handed, your seeking is not getting you what you really want. Real finding reveals the treasure buried within you. So when you hear a voice say, "Pilgrim, your search is ended," you may discover that the voice is your own.

All men should strive to learn before they die
what they are running from, and to, and why.

— JAMES THURBER

10

GOOD NEWS FOR PERFECTIONISTS

When weaving a blanket, an Indian woman leaves a flaw in the weaving of that blanket to let the soul out.

— **MARTHA GRAHAM**

A long time ago, in a galaxy far, far away, I developed a crush on a girl who worked in a local pet shop. When I went into the store, Becky and I would chat and laugh, and I felt a spark when we were together. I sensed that she was also attracted to me, and I fantasized about dating her. We were from different cultures and had different lifestyles, but still I hoped that we might have a relationship.

When Becky told me her birthday was coming up, I bought her a nice card and inscribed a poem. As I approached the pet store to deliver the card, my heart was pounding, and my palms grew sweaty. What if I professed my caring and she rejected me? So I did the thing that any able-bodied chicken would do: I stuffed the card under my shirt. I decided that I would start a conversation with Becky, and if she showed signs of interest or affection, I would give her the card. If she displayed no interest, I would play it safe and leave the store without putting myself on the line.

I found Becky at the cash register and said hello. That day she did not seem especially interested in connecting; she was pleasant, but not attentive. Disappointed, I started to leave. But as I stepped away, I felt a push back in her direction. I decided to take the plunge. I removed the card from under my shirt, went to the counter, told her "Happy birthday," and gave her the card.

Becky smiled politely, said "Thank you," put the card aside without opening it, and turned to the next customer without giving me a second look.

Shot down royally! I exited the store feeling utterly deflated. I had put my heart on the line and been rejected. Yet as I made my way to my car, another feeling began to overtake me: exhilaration. I experienced the deep joy of letting my affection shine—and that felt fantastic! I did what I had to do, and I was in integrity with myself. Ultimately it didn't matter whether or not I received a particular response. The true reward was in the expression.

A year later I was invited to speak at the Inside Edge, an empowerment group in Southern California. After I shared the story of my short-lived love affair, a fellow approached me and told me, "I loved your birthday-card story. I am putting together a book of inspiring stories, and I would really like to include yours. May I?"

"Sure," I told him. His name was Jack Canfield, and the following year I found my story in the first edition of *Chicken Soup for the Soul,* which became an international bestseller, with millions of copies in print. I later contributed several more stories to subsequent editions of the wildly popular series.

I did not get a date with Becky, but my experience with her made me a #1 *New York Times* best-selling author. Shot down briefly, but shot into space permanently—not a bad deal after all!

Everything that happens ultimately serves us. An experience might not appear to be perfect according to the ego's plan, but it may be supremely perfect according to Spirit's plan.

If something doesn't fit into your idea of how things should

> Creativity is allowing yourself to make mistakes. Art is knowing which ones to keep.
> — Scott Adams

go, step back and see how it might fit into a bigger idea of how things should go. You might find that, despite appearances, everything is working in your favor.

Where Perfection Lives

"I used to think I was a perfectionist," a friend of mine confessed. "I was constantly finding flaws and errors that other people overlooked. If ninety-nine aspects of a job were well done and one wasn't, I would point out that one. But now I realize I was really an *imperfectionist*. If I was a perfectionist, I would have found perfection everywhere I looked."

The enlightened Japanese practice of *wabi sabi* embraces a broader idea of perfection than "factory-fresh." *Wabi sabi* capitalizes on errors rather than bemoaning them. In Japan when a vase breaks, the owner mends it by filling the crack with gold. The Japanese believe that when something has been damaged, it takes on richer character and becomes more valuable.

Can you see the gold in your errors, wrinkles, and problems? Can you celebrate *all* parts of you, in-cluding the ones that do

> Welcome is every organ and attribute of me [. . .]
> Not an inch nor a particle of an inch is vile, and none shall be less familiar than the rest.
> — Walt Whitman

not seem attractive or worthwhile from society's point of view? Have you heard that "gray is the new blonde"? Can you honor your contributions rather than condemning your mistakes?

Perfection not only has space for imperfection—it depends on it.

The Supermodel's Secret

My friends Tom and Laura have had a rewarding marriage for many years. Like most couples, they have their issues. One day Laura confided in me, "I thought about leaving Tom because he was not all I hoped he would be. Then I realized that I have no right to demand perfection from him because I cannot offer perfection *to* him."

No one can offer absolute perfection. Yet we can offer the perfect version of ourselves at any given moment. To do so we must embrace our humanness. The little statues of man and wife on top

> Even I don't wake up looking like Cindy Crawford.
> — Cindy Crawford

of wedding cakes have no pimples, but they have no life. They are made of plastic and will never live or breathe. When the wedding day is over, they will be cast into the trash. When your real-life wedding is done, your relationship takes on greater life . . . a journey between two human beings seeking to bring forth the best in each other (with occasional appearances of the worst).

Quit judging yourself by an impossible standard. Let yourself be what you are, who you are, where you are, as you are. Relationships exist be-tween people who express

> A friend is someone who sees through you and still enjoys the view.
> — Wilma Askinas

both divinity and humanity. Respect the balance of the two and you have a good shot at happiness.

A Simple Choice

"There are three kinds of people," says Ram Dass. "Those who say, 'not enough'; those who say, 'too much'; and those who say, 'just right.'" Actually there are only two types, since too much of one thing is not enough of another. So all seeing boils down to the simple choice between grievance and gratitude.

While you believe that you have many choices before you, the only one that really matters is the type of vision you use, the shape of the lens through which you filter life. Every thought you think, word you speak, and action you perform proceeds from either love or fear. Begin to notice whether the choice you are currently making is dictated by love or by fear. Then choose love, or any variation of it, and you will have made the only choice worth making.

It is wise to reach for perfection, but unwise to beat yourself up if you do not attain it. Striving for perfection creates excellence, but addiction to it creates frustration and depression. There is perfection in the journey that is not obvious until the end of the journey. Enjoy the process and let your flaws become your friends. Your beauty is not earned by changing. It is revealed by accepting all of you. When you embrace the human, you liberate the divine.

I have an everyday religion that works for me.
Love yourself first and everything else falls into line.

— **Lucille Ball**

11

WHO VALIDATES YOU?

*I do not care so much what I am to
others as I care what I am to myself.
I want to be rich by myself, not by borrowing.*

— **MICHEL DE MONTAIGNE**

I received a voice-mail message from a friend who is a massage therapist at a luxury hotel. "Call me," she requested excitedly. "I have to tell you about my brush with greatness."

When I returned her call and ask her what had happened, she told me, "I massaged Dustin Hoffman today."

Well, that was cool. Yet something about her phrase "my brush with greatness" did not sit well with me.

"Dustin Hoffman is a great actor," I told her. "But when you say 'my brush with greatness,' it sounds as if he is great and you are not, and you were lucky to touch greatness for a moment. In my opinion you are just as great as he is. You are an outstanding massage therapist and an awesome person. Who knows, maybe after his massage he phoned a friend and reported, 'I have to tell you about my brush with greatness.'"

⌒

Many of us believe that greatness lives outside of us, and if we can somehow import it, we too will be great. We believe that we are empty or lacking and others are whole, and we can offset our lack by getting some of their light to shine into our darkness. So we emulate them, idolize them, rub shoulders with them, drop their names, get our photos taken with them, and build our identity around theirs, hoping that the power, beauty, wealth, fame, love, or happiness they possess will become our own. Yet when we seek to live in reflected glory, we miss the glory we already own.

You are already a star in your own right, and no one outside you can add to your brilliance. Instead of importing greatness from the outer world, tap into the magnificence you already own and are, and bring it forth. You do not need to brush with greatness; you simply need to brush *from* greatness.

Heartthrobs and Hot Rods

Do you need any person, object, or ideology to give you a sense of self-worth? Does your experience of validation come from others, or yourself?

Teenagers, for example, are prone to seek to borrow identity. Girls develop a crush on the latest heartthrob, and they wallpaper their bedrooms with photos of their idol. While such adoration is innocent enough, it sets up the dynamic: "If I can just fill my world with him, I will feel beautiful and lovable." Later the girl as a young woman chooses a fantasy husband who could not possibly live up to Prince Charming's résumé. When his human foibles come to the fore, she becomes disappointed, frustrated, and angry. Many couples part at such a juncture, while others use the shift from idol to real person to build an authentic relationship between two human beings. They do not seek to derive worth *from* the relationship; instead, they bring worth *to* it, which makes the difference between disaster and fulfillment.

Young men play out the same dynamic with cars. The guy with the coolest car gets the hottest girl. So the fellow spends all of his money on a custom candy-apple-painted car with glimmering wheels, augmented lifters, purple lights flashing around the license plate, and a sound system with bass booms you can hear in Antarctica—all in hopes of attracting a girl who will be impressed by his (hot) rod.

Fortunately, in spite of all of our attempts to import worth, life disrobes phoniness, rewards authenticity, and leads us back to our innate splendor. When Mr. Hot Rod finds a girlfriend who loves him just for his car, he feels even emptier because he as a person is absent from the equation of love in the relationship. He has also set up his relationship to self-destruct by attracting someone who is equally enamored of an object.

Whenever there is an agreement that objects or idols are more valuable than people, despair must enter and point us back to who we are, not what we own. The universe is constantly, lovingly, persistently, patiently nudging us (sometimes with a sledgehammer) back to the one essential truth that makes us happy:

You are valuable and lovable for who and what you are.
Nothing outside you can add to or detract from your inherent wholeness.

Your True Quest

The need for others to validate you is really a quest for self-validation. If you know your worth, you do not need other people to affirm it. If you do not recognize your worth, all the validation in the world will not fill the void you perceive. Your worthiness depends on nothing outside you, and everything inside you. Consider this bumper sticker: GOD LOVES YOU, AND THERE'S NOTHING YOU CAN DO ABOUT IT.

Many people spend a lot of time, energy, effort, and money trying to prove themselves to others. They amass degrees, corporate clout, trivial data, sex appeal, celebrity friends, and trendy jargon, all in hopes of impressing other people and demonstrating their wisdom, power, beauty, and achievement. Yet the proving game is booby-trapped from the start. When you begin with the assumption that you are not enough, and if you can just get enough people (or one significant person) to recognize that you are enough, you set yourself up to lose, because your initial premise was faulty. The more you try to prove yourself, the more you need to prove.

In the movie *Cool Runnings* (based on a true story), an unlikely team from Jamaica enters the Olympic bobsled contest. On the eve of their competition, one of the team members is troubled. When the coach asks him what is the matter, he explains that he will be ashamed if the team goes home without a medal. The coach tells him that if he is not good enough without a medal, he will not be good enough *with* a medal.

No medal can make you more than you already are, and no lack of a medal can make you less than you already are. Kudos from the outer world are fun, but not necessary. Self-acknowledgment is the most valuable trophy you can place on your soul's mantel. Either you have inner peace or no peace. As you cultivate the knowledge of your intrinsic worth, you cease to be the slave of outer opinion and you source your life from your soul.

> It is not titles that honor men, but men that honor titles.
> — Niccolò Machiavelli

Get a Faith-Lift

I saw a television news story on "The Human Barbie," a woman who has undergone more than a hundred cosmetic surgeries at a cost of over a million dollars. When the interviewer asked her why she had gone to so much trouble and expense to look like a doll, she explained, "When I was not so pretty, I went to parties and men dissed me. Now I take great pleasure in dissing them." How much time, trouble, and money could this woman have saved simply by knowing her beauty and worth?

Cosmetic surgeries can be helpful if they improve your self-image and confidence. The better you feel about yourself, the more effective you will be. Before submitting to the knife, just check your motivation. If you approach your nips, tucks, and enhancements with a creative, self-honoring intention, enjoy the adventure. If you believe that they will make you something you are not and gain you love or approval, tread carefully. Consider, instead, getting an attitude-lift.

Real beauty is an energy you exude from within. I know many women and men who might not be considered attractive from a glamour-magazine standpoint, but they radiate such zest for life that everyone loves them and wants to be around them. My friend Elsita was 89 years old when I met her. She had such tremendous charisma that everyone in the community vied to be in her presence. I used to invite Elsita to be a guest lecturer at my Life Mastery Training programs. She would tell spicy stories about her life, recite from memory poetry she wrote at the outset of World War I, and reveal her beauty secrets to the group. (Her skin was hardly wrinkled.)

Elsita explained, "Every morning I stroke cream on my face with the affirmation 'Beauty, beauty, beauty . . . love, love, love . . . joy, joy, joy." Elsita's secret was not the cream, but the affirmation, which penetrated deep into her cells. Everyone loved Elsita not because she was a beauty queen, but because love oozed from her pores. That made her a *real* beauty queen.

⌒

A Course in Miracles asks us to remember, "I have a kingdom I must rule." That kingdom is not a geographical domain; it is the realm of the mind and heart.

The real shift you seek is not geographical, but attitudinal. When you see yourself from the perspective that God sees you—whole, perfect, and beautiful—you can drop your quest to become worthy. Your true value is built into you.

Can you remember who you were, what you knew, and how you felt before you were taught that you had to earn validation? When you reclaim that crucial memory, all the people whose approval you sought will be unimportant, for you have gained approval from the only person who matters.

12

WHERE FEW
HAVE GONE
BEFORE

Don't ask what the world needs.
Ask what makes you come alive, and go do it.
Because what the world needs is people who have come alive.

— **HOWARD THURMAN**

When a reporter asked child tennis prodigy Jennifer Capriati, "Would you like to be the next Chris Evert?" she answered, "No, I would like to be the first Jennifer Capriati."

Such confidence in one's unique gift is rare in a world obsessed with comparison. From an early age, you were taught that your value is measured against the achievements of others; that life is a competition and a popularity contest; and that the more you fulfill externally prescribed standards, the more successful you will be.

None of this is true.

Fully embracing your enoughness requires absolute confidence in your distinctive self. Survival of the fittest does not mean that the guy with the biggest muscles wins. It means that those who fit in the best win.

> Comparison is the thief of joy.
> — attributed to Dwight Edwards

There is more to fitting in than owning the latest designer alligator-skin bag. The real "fit" is into your own skin. The more you trust and express your unique gifts, the more reward those gifts will bring you.

The purpose of everything in creation is to express its true nature. A dog exists to express dogness, a tree exists to express treeness, and you exist to express youness. Dogs are happiest when they are doing dog things. If you try to force a dog to act like a cat, it will never live up to the task. *It's not supposed to.* All a dog needs to know is how to be a dog. *All you need know is how to be you.*

Whose Permission Do You Need?

You are in integrity when the life you live on the outside matches who you are on the inside.

You are out of integrity—*dis*integrated—when you attempt to be or do something you are not. When you believe you need the permission of others to do what you would like to do, you set yourself up for disappointment, frustration, and resentment.

> Man is the only creature who refuses to be what he is.
> — Albert Camus

When you recognize that the only permission you need is your own, you break free of the addiction to social approval and experience the freedom of authentic confidence.

The film *Trembling Before G-d* chronicles the lives of several gay and lesbian Orthodox Jews struggling to reconcile their sexual preference with the religion's edict against homosexuality. In the documentary, a fellow named Michael sought counsel from many

> Comparisons do ofttime great grievance.
> — John Lydgate

different rabbis, hoping to find one who would approve of his gay predilection. None would. One rabbi told Michael how to "cure" homosexuality: wrap a rubber band around your wrist, and whenever you feel a gay impulse, snap the rubber band.

Eventually Michael realized that his religion, or at least the people he spoke to within it, was never going to give him permission to be homosexual. Then Michael had a huge "Aha!" He gave *himself* the permission he sought. He came to peace with his truth, and took back his power from those to whom he had ascribed it. He ceased to compare himself with the standard others had set for him, and he decided that he was good enough regardless of who approved of him or who didn't.

If you use other people's rules as a yardstick for your worth, you will become confused and depressed. No one has the right or power to prescribe your life for you. If people try to shame or motivate you by comparing you negatively to others, that is *their* issue. If you feel guilty or less-than as a result of their insinuation, that is *your* issue. If you are secure within yourself, their attempts will not distract you from your own path; they might, in fact, strengthen your faith in your choice by virtue of the

> When you finally trust yourself, you will know how to live.
> — Johann Wolfgang von Goethe

contrast they highlight. In such a case, you can thank and bless people who try to influence you—not because you should buy the life they are selling, but because they are helping you discover who you really are and what you want. Then you can walk your own path with self-assurance that runs far deeper than social approval.

Compelling Self-Confidence

A few months after my friend Susan had been dating Lee, he told her that he was going away for the weekend. "What are you doing?" she asked.

"I'm going to San Francisco to see my girlfriend," he answered.

Susan replied, "Okay, call me when you get back."

Lee was astonished by Susan's response, since he had been with women before who would have upbraided him for revealing such intentions.

Upon Lee's return from San Francisco, he told Susan, "I've been doing some thinking. I care about you a lot more than the woman I visited. I would like to have a committed relationship with you." Lee went on to tell Susan that he was impressed by the confidence she displayed when he told her he was going to visit another lady. "I have never known a woman who trusted so deeply," he confessed.

"I figured that if it was right for us to be together, we would be," Susan replied. "If not, why make a fuss?"

A year later Lee and Susan were married. They have remained together for many years, raised a beautiful family, and enjoy working together in a New York counseling practice. "The day Susan sent me off with 'Call me when you get back' was a turning point in our relationship," Lee told me. "Her statement set a tone of visionary confidence that has raised the bar for me and founded our relationship in love and respect."

I am not suggesting that you simply say yes to anything your partner wants to do or put up with abuse in a relationship. I *am* suggesting that when you have confidence in yourself, your partner, your relationship, and life, you establish a standard that will create results far more rewarding than those you get when you don't believe in the exceptional worth you bring to the table of life.

Unique on the Shelf

After my first book, *The Dragon Doesn't Live Here Anymore,* was published, I went to a bookstore for the thrill of seeing it on the shelf. There I found it between books by Chopra and Dyer. As I surveyed the array of self-help books on display, I was stunned to find many excellent tomes by numerous popular authors on subjects similar to what I had written about. I was really glad that

I hadn't gone to the bookstore before I wrote the book—I would have been so intimidated that I never would have written it! I would have concluded that everything about the subject had already been written.

As I thought about it further, I realized that my book was unique not for the subject matter, but for *my perspective* on the subject matter. I was writing in a voice that had never been recorded before, styled by my singular experiences and viewpoint. So it was for Chopra, Dyer, and everyone else who has ever written. And so it is with you. You have nothing new to say—no one does—but you have a fresh way of saying it, which will appeal to the audience that matches your perspective. Never let yourself be intimidated by giants. Every giant once stood where you now stand, and you have the right and power to stand among them.

> Today you are you! That is truer than true!
> There is no one alive who is you-er than you!
> — Dr. Seuss

The Unsaturated Market

One of the most common complaints I hear from people who set out to establish a business or create a product or service is: "The market is saturated." Where I live on Maui, many people are either massage therapists or Realtors (and many are both!). When I ask some of them how they are doing, they shrug and tell me about how many people in their profession are all vying for the same pool of clients. Meanwhile some of those professionals are thriving gloriously. The massage therapist I see has more work than she can handle, and I had dinner with a Realtor who just sold a $27 million home. One has to wonder how these individuals are doing so well in a "saturated market."

The answer is twofold:

— First, we each live in the economy equivalent to our own consciousness. If you believe the market is saturated and clients are few, the market will be saturated for you. But if you recognize the value of what you have to offer, follow your passion, express your talent, sincerely seek to serve, and live in integrity, you will attract quality clients—and plenty of them. There is no such thing as *"the* economy" or *"the* market." Many economies exist simultaneously, and you live in the one that matches your mind-set. There are always people who thrive in a bad economy, and people who flounder in a good economy. So quit talking about "the economy" and create your own.

— Second, as Ernest Holmes declared, "There is room at the top." It is possible for many people to succeed in the same profession—if you get over the notion of "limited available good" and competition for it. This sounds like sacrilege to a society steeped in the belief in finite good—but remember that you are claiming *radical* contentment. If you think and act like everyone else, you will get the same results everyone else is getting. If you think and act uniquely, you will get unique results. There is room at the top for you if you are willing to claim it.

Boldly Go

The familiar voice-over introduction to the *Star Trek* series declares that the starship *Enterprise*'s mission is to boldly go where no one has gone before. So, too, must you go where no one has gone before. If you try to build your success on where others have gone before, you will be just another clone seeking glory by following a formula. If you can be true to your individual calling, you will pave the way for something never before experienced, and enhance the lives of many who follow the path you carve through the weeds you trample.

> To change one's life:
> 1. Start immediately.
> 2. Do it flamboyantly.
> 3. No exceptions.
> — attributed to William James

It's time to give up the comparison game. Use others for inspiration as role models, but do not cower in their shadow. You have your own niche in the grand scheme of creation. The market is not saturated, because you have a corner on the market of *you*. Do not compromise your wholeness by seeing yourself as less than others, or more. All share equally in the gifts of God. Happiness is not won or lost by comparison. It founds itself in your confidence to be precisely what you are and do what only you can do.

13

God Doesn't Owe, and Neither Do You

He [. . .] looks the whole world in the face,
For he owes not any man.

— **Henry Wadsworth Longfellow**

We live in a society where most people are in debt. Nearly everyone owes lots of money for credit-card bills, car payments, mortgages, and business investments. It is really, really rare that someone in our culture is solvent. Americans currently hold 609 million credit cards, or two for every man, woman, and child in the country. The total amount of personal debt in the United States is $16 trillion, including $14 trillion in mortgage debt and $2 trillion in credit-card debt. The average American home owner owes $200,000 to mortgage companies, and the average household owes $16,000 to credit-card companies. The national debt of the United States is $62 trillion, or $534,000 for every household in America. Forty percent of the U.S. revenue goes to pay off loans. No wonder people sport bumper stickers proclaiming: I OWE, I OWE, IT'S OFF TO WORK I GO.

Consequently, many people feel burdened by debt. They worry about paying their bills, borrow from one credit card to pay another, and make foolish or illicit deals in hopes of salvaging their finances. The number one cause of arguments in marriages is money. Our individual and collective consciousness about money and debt is crying out for healing.

While many people feel anxious or desperate about debt and money, there are ways to look at these dynamics that can empower you. Nothing is good or bad in and of itself; *perspective* determines joy or pain. Money is not the root of all evil. Fear is. If you can remove fear and guilt from your relationship with money, all financial transactions, including the experience of debt, will shift . . . and serve you.

The Identity Factor

Let's begin with a big-picture shift in your relationship with money. Most people who owe money over a length of time begin to think of themselves as a debtor. They develop the mind-set: *I owe, and I will always owe.* But "As a man thinketh, so shall he be." When you identify yourself as a debtor, you keep creating and attracting experiences that prove your identity. At some point the problem is less that you owe money, and more that you are entrenched in an identity as a debtor.

From a broader perspective, such an identity is false and runs contrary to who and what you really are. As a spiritual being, you are created in the image and likeness of God. Everything God is, you are; and everything God is not, you are not. When you say, "I owe" or "I am a debtor," you are suggesting that God owes or God is a debtor. This is not true about God, and it is not true about you.

In the world of human interaction, you may have run up debt, but on a broader dimension you are absolutely whole, solvent, and literally as rich as God. The entire universe is your estate, and all the good in it belongs to you. The experience of debt exists only at the surface level of existence. You and your life run so much deeper than your financial situation that what balance sheets say is relatively meaningless. Your spiritual balance sheet takes into account joy, happiness, and inner peace—not dollars. When you shift your vision from what your bank statement says to what your soul statement says, lack and despair dissolve, and abundance is the truth of your life.

If you examine the concept that God could owe, you can see how ludicrous the idea is. What would God owe? Why? To whom? What recourse would some illusory creditor have if God didn't pay? The entire idea is meaningless. All of nature functions on the principle of giving its gifts, not collecting from others. Creation is generous, happy just to be itself, and makes no demands. The sun does not hold the earth in debt; it simply delights to shine on it. Neither do the trees demand a return for the oxygen they provide. Debt exists only in the minds of people, never in nature.

If you would like to offset your identity as a debtor and the experiences that follow in its wake, use this affirmation:

God doesn't owe, and neither do I.

If you declare this statement and recognize its truth, your identity as a debtor will begin to dissolve and your life will mirror solvency, not debt . . . supply, not lack. You will think and feel differently about money, and you will see literal, material changes in your prosperity. When you change your mind, everything changes.

At this point you may say, "Well, that's a nice idea, but my landlord will not accept an affirmation in lieu of my rent. He prefers cash."

Yes, yes, understood. But remember that when you upgrade your mind-set, you set into motion dynamics that transform circumstances. All material change is preceded by consciousness change. The world is an effect more than a cause. This is why most lottery winners revert to their former level of wealth within a short time. Their minds do not have the capacity to hold or manage large sums, so the money goes away. By this same principle many millionaires have lost their net worth, but regained it and more because they live in a wealth mentality. Even though they may experience temporary setbacks, their mind-set re-mag-netizes wealth. The source of all wealth is a wealthy mind.

> Mind is the builder.
> — Edgar Cayce

If, while using this affirmation, you don't resonate with the concept of God, substitute "the universe," "life," or "well-being." Don't get hung up on the terminology. It is the *dynamic principle* that counts and works. Don't deny yourself the experience of suc-cess because in elementary school a nun slapped your open palm with a ruler. If *you* continue slapping your hand, she wins. If you open your palm to receive wealth, *you* win.

The way to move from debt to solvency is not simply to work harder or move money around. You achieve solvency and surplus by working smarter and moving your thoughts around.

Shining the Light on the Shadow

Financial debt is a symptom of a deeper psychological sense of debt. If you harbor a self-image of guilt or unworthiness, that belief often plays out in your financial life. Many people believe that they are defective and they do not deserve to have what they want. They feel they are less than other people and are indebted to them. They believe they do not have a right to be here and they need others to validate them. They give their power away to other people, and since money mirrors energy flow, currency flows away from them to others.

Religions instill and promulgate this sense of debt by preach-ing concepts of sin and unworthiness. They tell you that there was something wrong with you before you even emerged from the womb, and you are so intrinsically vile that you need an ex-ternal redeemer to offset your iniquity. A savior died for your sins, and you gain heaven by the intercession of someone more worthy than you. If you adopt such a belief, you will be playing psychological catch-up ball for your entire life. Since money reflects consciousness, you will forever be trying to catch up on your finances.

The cure for debt is to recognize that you deserve enough because you *are* enough. You were created whole and worthy, and so you remain. There is nothing about you that owes anything to anyone. If you can tap into your inherent enoughness, you will find your way out of debt. You are an abundant being living in an abundant universe. That is the truth about you and life. Everything else is a story you made up.

> You are a miracle, capable of creating in the likeness of your Creator. Everything else is only your own nightmare. . . . Only the creations of light are real.
> — *A Course in Miracles*

Just as you made up a story of debt (or you adopted one), you can make up a story of prosperity. The universe is willing and happy to prove your prosperity story, for that story is far closer to the truth about you than the debt yarn you spin. "Though I walk through the valley of the shadow of debt, I will fear no evil." Debt is but a shadow that momentarily obscures your vision of the sun. Just as the sun remains fully intact even if a cloud floats before it, abundance is real even if a momentary notion of lack blocks it. That thought takes the form of *I owe,* or *I am not enough.* Replace that notion with the affirmation *I am enough, and the universe is happy to provide for my needs,* and the cloud disappears.

Don't make dissolution of debt any more complicated than it needs to be. Healing is an inside job. Your current financial situation is the result of the thoughts you held in the past, and tomorrow's financial situation will be the result of the thoughts you launch today. The first step to expand your bank balance is to expand your mind. When mind changes, what's "mine" changes. *God doesn't owe, and neither do you.* That insight is a gift, not a loan, and you will never have to pay it back.

The One Thing You Can't Afford to Postpone

Another way to rise above a debt mentality is to find fulfillment right where you stand, no matter what your bank account says. Don't postpone joy until you are out of debt. Joy is the only thing you cannot afford to postpone.

Money is a paper game; it is not the source of happiness. It is an effect, not a cause. Many millions of people who do not have money are far happier than people who have lots of money. They find riches in simple things, and do not let their bank account rule their peace. There are also wealthy people who are happy— but they were happy before they had money. A *USA Today* survey asked wealthy people, "Which came first: success or happiness?" Sixty-five percent of respondents reported that happiness preceded success. In other words, happiness attracts success more powerfully than success attracts happiness. So money does not cause happiness or unhappiness. Outlook and attitude cause happiness or unhappiness.

Many corporations show debt on their financial statements, but they keep making money and paying their employees well. Airlines and department-store chains have filed bankruptcy statements, but continue to operate, business as usual, and even grow. Their executives do not pull their hair out because they are losing money on paper. Many such companies and their employees continue to thrive, and so can you.

Money is one thing. Life is another. If you think money is life, your life will go up and down with money. If you focus on joy in the present moment, money will assume its rightful place as one aspect of life, not all of it.

The Prosperity Pie

Consider that prosperity is a pie, or a pie-shaped graph, and money is one small slice of it. There are so very, very many slices of the prosperity pie that go far beyond money. You may be extremely wealthy in family, love, health, nature, music, inspiration, connection to a Higher Power, friends, stimulating ideas, sports and recreation, playtime with pets, fascinating hobbies, creativity, and on and on and on. All of these experiences are rock-solid forms of wealth, far more real and valuable than dollars in your hand. If you feel poor financially, consider all of the other ways that you are rich, and you will immediately experience lavish abundance.

Doing such an exercise will make you feel wealthy, yet it serves a broader purpose. Feeling prosperous will put you in the optimal position to attract money and other forms of abundance. The Law of Attraction posits that you attract more of whatever you focus on. If your dominant feeling is wealth, you will attract situations that mirror wealth. If your dominant experience is poverty, you will attract situations that reflect poverty. You are always manifesting, even when it appears that nothing is happening. Take care what your dominant feeling is, for that is the magnet that will draw equivalent people, events, and experiences into your world.

If you are worried about money, temporarily take your attention off the subject of money and give your attention to other forms of prosperity. When you

> A rising tide raises all the ships.
> — Source unknown

are absorbed in the experience of abundance in other areas of your life, you will amplify your ability to attract prosperity in your financial arena.

Solvent Now

You are spiritually solvent now. That is the only form of solvency that really matters. Erase debt from your mind and heart, and it will be erased from your balance sheet. Do not fall prey to "lack" thinking that immobilizes the masses, and do not accept any definition of yourself as owing. Jesus did not die to pay off your karmic debts. He lived, and lives, to demonstrate that you don't have any. God's idea of grace supersedes your idea of karma.

Do not be distracted by news of financial woe. There is nothing new about such news. News is based on drama, fear, illusion, and sensationalism. Create your own news and your own economy by virtue of your consciousness, independent of the economy that others create with *their* consciousness. Claim the wealth you were born to enjoy, which exists fully and freely right now.

God doesn't owe, and neither do you. Know it, believe it, and live it . . . and you will find that solvency is not an impossible dream, but a solid reality.

14

THE END
OF GUILT

You need not fear the Higher Court will condemn
you. It will merely dismiss the case against you.
There can be no case against a child of God.

— *A COURSE IN MIRACLES*

We are told in the book of Genesis that "a deep sleep" fell upon Adam. But nowhere in the Bible are we told that Adam ever woke up! In a sense, we are all still asleep, dreaming the illusions of separateness, loss, fear, shame, and death.

The weight that holds Adam's (and our) eyelids closed is guilt. This emotion, prevalent as it is, is not natural to a human being. It is entirely learned. Children have no concept of guilt. They live in innocence and freedom. Guilt is cast over the child at a young age like a dark, heavy, tattered, foul-smelling cloak passed down through generations, binding innocent souls in a burdensome cycle of apologetic living.

The journey to freedom does not require you to become any-thing you are not. It simply invites you to throw off illusions of limitation and return to the Garden of Eden you enjoyed before you learned to be afraid. As Swami Satchidananda noted, "We started off fine. Then we got de-fined. Now we are getting re-fined."

I had a revelation about guilt shortly after the terrorist attacks of September 11, 2001. Around that time, I flew to Australia to present a series of seminars. In the wake of the attacks, American airports were heavily militarized. I remember entering the Honolulu airport and shuddering to see soldiers in combat uniforms patrolling the terminals with submachine guns. Travelers were searched bodily while agents opened suitcases in public, examining intimate personal possessions. IDs were checked and re-checked. Everyone from children to senior citizens was suspicious; it seemed as if one had to disprove one's guilt before boarding an aircraft.

In Australia I had to take a domestic flight from Sydney to Melbourne. As I approached the Sydney airport, I felt anxious about going through the intense security screening to which I had become accustomed. To my astonishment, when I checked in for my flight, the agent did not even ask for my ID. After I told her my name, she smiled and handed me a boarding pass. As I made my way to my gate, the only security measure required was to pass through one metal detector, monitored by a few laid-back guards. I encountered no double-checking, searching, or disrobing. As I completed my minor screening process and boarded the airplane, I had the strangest feeling that I had somehow cheated or gotten away with something I did not deserve. The whole process seemed just too easy! I had nothing to hide, but still I felt somehow . . . guilty.

I had become so accustomed to being treated as a potential criminal or threat that when I was respected as innocent, that experience felt foreign to me. Suddenly I understood how all of us have been trained to feel guilty. We have been told for so long that there is something wrong with us that when we are treated as if there is something *right* with us, we can't quite relate to that experience, and we just wait to be "found out."

But there is nothing to be found out. While we have been taught that guilt is the truth and innocence the lie, *innocence* is the truth and guilt is the lie.

This indoctrination runs so deep on an emotional level that you are not likely to throw off such dense programming overnight. But a seed of this understanding can turn on a light that leads to the eventual undoing of guilt at the most fundamental layers of your being. That process is the most healing, liberating, and glorious of your life. If this idea sparks a vision of freedom in your soul, the process has already begun.

Open the Bowl

In the Hawaiian spiritual tradition, a newborn child is regarded as a "bowl of light." If you observe a little child radiating positive energy, you can see an angel close to heaven. She has not yet learned all the conditions she must fulfill to merit love. She is already in a state of love, and has no concept of having to earn it.

Yet there comes a day when society drops a rock into the bowl of light. The child learns self-criticism, shame, and the sense: *I must perform to deserve love.* Now the rock obscures some of the light the bowl is emitting. As time goes on, more rocks fall into the bowl: fear, mistrust, a sense of lack, competition, envy, anger. . . . Eventually there are so many rocks in the bowl that only a tiny trickle of light escapes. Behold millions of people commuting to work and walking the streets of our cities, their eyes darkened, shoulders bent, sadness and pain oozing from their pores. Their beautiful bowls of light have become filled with so many rocks of disappointment, pressure, and obligation that they seem more dead than alive.

How can you escape the plight of the zombie and restore the original light shining in your bowl? Begin to pay more attention to the sense of delight within you than the sense of guilt, and act on what makes you happy rather than what fear demands you to do. Take time each day to feed your soul. Associate with people you respect and enjoy. Make play, recreation, renewal, and family time as important as work. Follow your creative impulses. Laugh. Trust your intuition more than external dictates.

Identify the voice in your head that tells you that you are evil or worthy of punishment, and identify the voice that affirms your innocence and your right to be happy. Which feels better? Which would you choose as your guide to life? Guilt and fear are habits you developed,

> The critical voice is not your own.
> — Source unknown

and as such, they can be replaced by more rewarding patterns of thought and feeling. The habit of inner peace is easier to cultivate because it is your natural state. May your return be swift and easy.

End the Proving Game

If you do not know that you are already enough, nothing you do to become enough will make you enough. When you realize that you are enough, the self-proving game is over. I coached a woman named Donna who was very successful in business, but in pain emotionally and physically. Although she was the CEO of a thriving multinational company, her life was a frantic run on a treadmill to keep achieving more, more, and more.

As a child, Donna had taken piano lessons. During her practice sessions, her father, a very demanding man, sat beside her on the piano bench. He placed a 50-cent coin on the piano and told her, "If you play this piece without making any mistakes, you can keep the money." If not, he would withdraw the coin.

At age six Donna found it difficult to play the piano perfectly. She almost never won the coin. When she grew up and entered the business world, she carried this attitude into her work life: *You*

> Human beings are the only creatures on the planet who tell time and think they have to earn a living.
> — Buckminster Fuller

have to work very hard for a coin that you almost never receive. So Donna kept struggling to be perfect, but in her mind she never hit the mark. This belief led to an incessant quest for degrees, credentials, and approval. Although she had many such accolades, she was never satisfied with herself, so she experienced deep stress and the emotional and physical symptoms indicative of lack of self-worth.

During the period I coached Donna, she gradually let go of many of the overwhelming tasks she had taken on, she lost excess weight, and her health improved significantly. She grew happy, relaxed, and made life choices in alignment with her joy. She could achieve this only when she stopped trying to prove herself, and began to find beauty and worth in herself just as she was.

Fraud Guilt

In his book *Authentic Success,* Dr. Robert Holden illuminates the dynamics behind *Fraud Guilt,* the feeling that "if you knew the truth about me, you would discover that I am a phony and you would reject me."

Most people experience some degree of Fraud Guilt. We believe that we have somehow fooled people into liking us, and that at a core level we are not the person they think we are. Our real self, we sense, is far inferior to our social image.

A survey was done among CEOs of Hollywood's top motion-picture studios. When they were asked, "What do you most fear?" the most prevalent answer was: "I fear that people will find out that I don't really know what I am doing." The irony of this response was that these executives really *did* know what they were doing. Even while they doubted themselves, they were turning out blockbusters. Meanwhile, that little voice of darkness kept nagging them and calling them phony.

Who was the real phony? *A Course in Miracles* tells us that "all defenses do what they would defend" against. The voice that calls you a fraud *is* the fraud—not you. The real you is magnificent and substantial. Your self-image as a phony is the liar.

Another name for Fraud Guilt is "inadequacy hypnosis." I like this term because it reveals that our sense of not-enoughness is but a hypnosis to which we have succumbed. When so many people believe there is something wrong with them, the mass agreement creates an illusion that is easy to fall into and hard to get out of. Yet each of us must escape from this dark dream, because it is foreign to our nature. The moment we awaken, all the illusions the dream engendered dissolve with it.

The pathetic voice of Fraud Guilt may become especially fierce when you are on the threshold of creating success, or when you have just done so. The closer you come to claiming your true power and happiness, the louder that nasty bugger will rant. Such resistance is a positive sign, for it indicates that you are breaking free of the prison in which guilt has held you captive. How do you overcome this ranting maniac? Simply notice this voice and keep moving ahead. Address it like a frightened child and explain to it that you are a good person, successful at your chosen endeavors for good reason. Tell it that it doesn't need to worry about your being exposed. The best thing that could happen to you would be to be completely exposed, for in the light of full exposure you would discover that everything you thought you needed to hide was a trick of fear. In uncharted territory you discover your greatest self.

> The dogs bark, but the caravan moves on.
> — Arab proverb

Who Invented Guilt?

A long time ago it was discovered that if you can get someone to feel guilty, you can control that person. Guilt is synonymous with fear of punishment, and those who fear punishment will do practically anything to avoid it, even if the punishment is not merited or actually forthcoming. Sometimes the *threat* of punishment is as effective, or even more effective, than the punishment itself. Ultimately *self*-punishment is more effective than punishment by the outer world. This is all that guilt is.

Since guilt first infiltrated the human psyche, billions of people and societal institutions have used it as a tool to manipulate and control others. Some religions have honed it to a fine science. (It is said: "The Jews invented guilt, and the Catholics perfected it.") While elements of religion bring people closer to God, guilt is not one of them. Guilt operates in a manner diametrically opposed to the true purpose of religion, for it leaves people feeling alienated from themselves and even hating God or religion.

It does not matter who invented guilt, and it certainly does not serve us to blame or seek revenge against those who perpetrate it. "We are protagonists and the authors of our own drama," author Rebecca McClen Novick states. "It is up to us; there is no one left to blame. Neither the 'system,' nor our leaders, nor our parents. We can't go out and hang the first amoeba."

If you have been sullied or plagued by guilt or shame, waste no time on collaring the perpetrators, and *do whatever it takes to get free.* If you find yourself in a burning building, you don't have time to analyze where the fire started. Just get out. Don't delay awakening by studying the darkness. Step into the light.

The Choice for Innocence

A Course in Miracles teaches that any choice motivated by guilt will not take you anywhere you really want to go. Whenever you act from a mind-set of fear or guilt, your results will backfire, and you will have to return to the crossroads and choose innocence. The universe is benevolent in never rewarding guilt and always rewarding love. This code runs contrary to what you might conclude from watching morbid news broadcasts, but the foundation upon which the universe rests runs far deeper than the media would have you know.

Guilt is an interpretation, not a fact. At any moment you can reinterpret any event through the eyes of innocence rather than guilt, grace rather than karma. When you see through the eyes of innocence, you liberate yourself and everyone you encounter. When you filter events through the lens of guilt, you condemn yourself and the world. The Crucifixion was not an act that occurred once. It recurs every time you incriminate or punish yourself or another. Neither was the Resurrection a singular event. It recurs every time you release yourself or another. Each new day is an opportunity to be raised from the tomb of fear.

Guilt will tell you there is no end to it, but love will tell you that this feeling was never justified from the start. If there is any purpose to guilt, it is to highlight the power and exhilaration of freedom *from* it.

Perhaps future generations, hopefully wiser than those we have known, will look back on our time and ponder it with the same curiosity and compassion that we hold for past eras of slavery and despotism. If you wish to depose political tyrants, begin by removing internal tyrants. Daily we must heal thoughts and feelings of fear, alienation, and divisiveness.

When you come to peace with yourself, you will come to peace with the world.

Ancient Hatred and Present Love

I met a fellow who was glowing. "I just came from a therapy group, and I learned a new and exciting technique!" he exclaimed. "It's called 'shame reduction.'"

I had to scratch my head. To me, "shame reduction" sounded a lot like forgiveness. There is nothing new about forgiveness, or our deep need to find it. Mercy has been around as long as guilt has required it

> The holiest of all the spots on earth is where an ancient hatred has become a present love.
> — *A Course in Miracles*

for healing. Yet shame reduction—aka forgiveness—*is* new and exciting every time you apply it. When you come to the fork in the road where you have traditionally chosen guilt and you choose freedom instead, the heavens rejoice and a breath of relief ripples through the world.

Each day is a series of opportunities to end guilt, beginning with your own. Every person you meet, every situation, every perceived error is an invitation to "reframe" in favor of innocence. If you are wondering about your purpose in a relationship, a career, or life, the answer is to choose healing where you once perceived vengeance. Then the world will become new because you have finally become a friend to yourself.

15

How Easy Can It Get?

Yesterday I dared to struggle. Today I dare to win.

— **Bernadette Devlin**

Standing before the staggering Mayan temples at Chichén Itzá and Tulum, our tour guide told us that the Maya, although sophisticated in astronomy and mathematics, regularly offered blood sacrifices to appease their gods. "The Maya feared that if they did not make sacrifices to the sun god, the sun would not rise the next morning," the guide explained. "In times of drought, they sought to appease the rain god with multiple sacrifices."

Primitive and abhorrent as such practices seem to us today, the mind-set of sacrifice is still very much alive. Many of us believe we must sacrifice something we value to gain something else we want. We believe that struggle, sweat, and conflict are required to make strides in our career; we must deny our joy so others can have theirs; and, under a "No pain, no gain" mentality, if we are not suffering, we have it too easy. While we are not sacrificing whole bodies, as the Maya did, we forfeit our emotions, our happiness, and often our health. Our sacrifices do not execute us in one horrid moment, as they did the Maya, but they strangle us over time, a bit more each day. We fall not under the knife of the shaman, but under the whip of ongoing self-recrimination.

> How much easier is self-sacrifice than self-realization!
> — Eric Hoffer

The belief that struggle is more valuable than joy pervades nearly every domain of human endeavor. Guilt is an insidious shape-shifter that tailors itself to the path you currently walk. A psychiatrist friend of mine reports that her "New Age" clients feel guilty if they have a problem or get sick, since they have been told that you should feel good and be happy all the time; if you feel otherwise, it is your fault. Many corporations demand employees to carry a burdensome load of projects and forgo personal renewal; in Japan, many people work until 8, 9, or 10 every evening.

> Attempt no more to win through losing nor to die to live.
> — A Course in Miracles

The unspoken rule is that if you go home before your boss, you should feel guilty. Although Japanese employees are afforded 18 vacation days/holidays a year, most people take no more than 8, since any greater number indicates that you are lazy.

A woman who grew up in Communist Russia told me that citizens were expected to dedicate their lives to the party cause, with strict punishments for stepping out of line. The more she explained, the more Communism sounded like a religion.

When guilt creeps into the human psyche, its demands for blood surface at every turn. One of my coaching clients confessed, "I can turn anything into boot camp."

When the Maya labored under the illusion that sacrifices were causing the sun to rise, superstition eclipsed science. If that culture suspended sacrifices for any length of time, they would have discovered there was no relationship between the loss of life and the gain of sunlight. They would have found that the sun is happy to shine on all things unconditionally, no payment required.

If we suspended our belief in personal sacrifice, we too might discover that life is happy to empower us without exacting a fee.

Institutions steeped in fear, competition, and addiction to power may demand sacrifices, but nothing else in the natural world does. Life takes no joy in your loss; to the contrary, the heart of God cries when *you* do. If you and I could realize that death does not keep the sun rising, we would find that our blood serves us far better in our veins than spilled.

Recovering from Hardaholism

Were you taught any or all of the following beliefs?

- Life is a struggle, and if things come easy, you are cheating.

- Success is the result of painful work and self-sacrifice.

- When you receive good things, you are depriving someone else.

- Money is evil, and rich people go to hell.

- You should feel guilty if you receive any kind of pleasure, especially sex.

- Massages, hot tubs, vacations, and room service are self-indulgent.

- Asking for what you want is selfish.

- Doing what you want is arrogant.

- You are intruding on life by being here, and you need to apologize for your existence.

If any or all of these beliefs apply to you, you qualify as a *hardaholic:* someone who is addicted to doing everything the hard way. As illuminated by "easy learner" Anne Sermons Gillis, hardaholics worship at the altar of struggle and find a way to make simple decisions painful and complicated. Fear, worry, and conflict accompany all projects and relationships. Hardaholics have to constantly fight for their good, and hardly ever receive it. Life is an uphill battle they can never win.

Hardaholics do not realize that struggle is a choice, and there is an easier route if you are willing to take it. Suffering is not of the will of God. When you realize that God wants only your happiness, you love yourself as God loves you. Parents who love their children guide them *away* from pain, never more deeply into it. Universal intelligence never intended for you to fight your way through life.

How do you overcome hardaholism? Begin by questioning your belief that what you find hard *has* to be hard. Ask yourself, "How much of this is hard because of the situation, and how much is hard because I am seeing it as hard or I am making it hard?" You might be surprised to find that struggle is the offspring of perception and projection more than reality. Then ask yourself, "If I were willing to let this be easy, how would I be approaching this differently?" If you can discover a vantage point even a bit freer than the one you have been holding, you will take a significant step from struggle to peace.

Cruising Altitude

When an airplane encounters turbulence, the pilot seeks another altitude. If the aircraft tries to buck through the resistance, it will be racked with chop. So the pilot rises to a higher altitude or drops to a lower one where the skies are clear and navigable. Eventually the plane will pass the turbulent zone and be able to reclaim its normal cruising altitude.

When most people hit turbulence in their lives, they try to buck through it. They do not consider shifting to another altitude. If you are locking horns in a relationship, for example, scan for another level at which resolution is available. Find a frequency more aligned with solutions, and invite the other person to join you there. Even if he or she doesn't go there with you, establish yourself in the frequency of "solution," where you will have the greatest strength to draw the other person to meet you. When you live in the answer more than the question, resolution will manifest.

I love the expression "sweet spot." Whenever you are looking for an answer or trying to settle a dispute, there is a way that can work for everyone. I experience this phenomenon when training life coaches. Setting a fee is usually a challenging issue for a new life coach, likewise in many professions. If a coach tells me that she does not know how much to charge, I ask, "How does $50 feel?"

The coach shakes her head and replies, "That feels kind of low."

"Okay, how about $100?" I ask.

"I think that's a bit much," comes the response.

"How about $75?"

A smile comes over the coach's face. "That feels right to me."

I never tell a coach how much to charge. Some feel comfortable with $25 a session, and others might find their sweet spot at $150. There is no absolute rule. Every coach and professional must find his own sweet spot and set a fee that feels peaceful for him.

You, too, must find your proper cruising attitude or sweet spot in your relationship, home, career, and body. If you are experiencing turbulence, keep scanning. When you find your sweet spot, you will know it and your soul will say, *"Ahhhh."*

Role Models of Ease

Another way to overcome a struggle mentality is to find and focus on role models of ease. When I began to organize seminars, I felt quite stressed handling the event logistics. I worried about everything getting done and wanted all the participants to have all their needs met and be satisfied with the program. My anxiety diminished the quality of my teaching, and when the program was over, I felt exhausted.

Around that time I attended a huge psychology convention at Princeton University. Just before the program's opening lecture, I noticed the conference director chatting with someone outside the auditorium. The director looked extraordinarily relaxed, laughing and obviously enjoying himself.

That moment I realized that stress is not a condition; it is a choice. I had been feeling overwhelmed servicing 30 participants for a weekend retreat, while this fellow did not appear at all flustered about servicing 2,000 professionals at an internationally renowned convention. That man became my role model for ease, and his image has served me for many years. If I ever start to feel tense about organizing anything, I envision him laughing on the steps of the lecture hall. I don't remember his name, but his gift to me has lasted a lifetime.

At another time, some friends and I rented a cabin in the extinct volcanic crater of Haleakala National Park on Maui. To get to the cabin, we had to hike down a long switchback trail. During our hike, the weather was cloudy and misty, with practically zero visibility. Finally we arrived at the cabin and spent several glorious days in this sacred, pristine environment.

On our way hiking back up the mountainside, the weather was sunny and clear. To my shock, I discovered that the switchback was carved into the side of a steep cliff with a sheer thousand-foot drop-off! Although the path was wide enough to easily traverse, I began to feel anxious and unsteady. After a while I experienced what resembled a panic attack. I felt immobilized, and I feared to move forward or back.

Just then I noticed another hiker walking down the trail toward us. She was having a grand time enjoying the expansive view, her step light and her face shining. This woman was on the same trail I was, yet she was not fearful at all; to the contrary, she was in a state of ecstasy. I realized that if she was having such a good time, perhaps I could, too. I took a deep breath and tried to see the journey through her appreciative eyes, not the fearful interpretation that had smothered me. When I tried on for size the idea of enjoying the hike, I felt a significant shift. I continued on my way, panic lifted, feeling more relaxed and confident.

You can dissolve stress by considering how someone you respect would handle your situation. Think of someone who stays in the flow of life and does not get uptight. Then imagine how he or she would be acting in the circumstance you find distressing. How does she hold her body? What is the expression on his face? How would she be speaking? What would he be feeling?

As you attune to this person's easygoing energy, you touch the place inside you that is capable of relaxing about your task. Then, when you are in the midst of your challenging situation, act as if you are that person. You may be surprised by how a situation that once felt overwhelming can become doable and even fun.

How Much Do You Need to Work?

You probably have an idea of how much you need to work to get a job done or to earn a good salary. Is it 40, 60, or 80 hours a week? Do you need to forgo family dinners, weekends, vacations, and time with your loved ones? Do you need to say yes to your boss when you are aching to say no? Are you required to attend boring meetings and social functions with self-centered wind-bags? Do you have to force yourself to laugh at lame jokes, and put up with sarcasm, gossip, and repetitive war stories? When you get home, are you too tense or tired to make love with your spouse? Has work replaced your life?

If so, would you be open to the idea that you can work less and still achieve excellent results and significant income? Consider, for example, Hay House, the publisher of this book and many other self-improvement books and producer of inspirational seminars. Based on founder Louise L. Hay's philosophy of kindness to self, Hay House embraces a more relaxed attitude toward work than most corporations. Hay House employees have a four-day work-week, Monday through Thursday, from 7:00 A.M. to 5:30 P.M., with flexible and generous lunchtimes. The atmosphere in the company is light and casual; employees' offices and cubicles are decorated with festive personal photos and mementos, and laughter is heard often. The company retains employees for many years, and is generally free of the kind of competition, fear, and backbiting I have observed in other corporate environments.

If you think along more traditional lines, you might expect that such an easygoing organization would suffer for its relaxed demeanor. To the contrary, Hay House is a hugely successful publisher with frequent *New York Times* bestsellers, offices on five continents, and an impressive array of seminars with high attendance. Employees are committed to their jobs and creating excellent products. The absence of the "whip" in this company does not defeat the bottom line, but rather enhances it.

Another company of note is a software firm named Motek, celebrated in an airline-magazine article as "the best company to work for in the world—period." Motek employees must take at least a three-week vacation each year, for which they receive a $5,000 travel benefit, and they also get two weeks in paid holidays. Innovative CEO Ann S. Price sends everyone home at 5 P.M. without laptops, and the doors are closed on weekends. Ten-year company employees get a luxury leased automobile. The firm's revenue per employee tops competing firms by 10 to 25 percent. Motek proves that rest, relaxation, and fun are as vital ingredients for success as hard work.

Musician Karen Drucker spent many years performing for weddings and corporate meetings. She could sing a mean "Feelings" and draw tears with "Evergreen." Eventually Karen grew tired of the scene and yearned to compose and perform songs with more meaning for people who were sober and actually listening to her. One day a bride's mother viciously laid into Karen because she wasn't playing enough polkas. "That was it," Karen recounts. "I knew there must be a better way to earn a living."

Karen cut loose from her career as she knew it and launched herself into composing original music with uplifting lyrics and self-styled melodies. Before long she became a popular performer at New Thought churches and conferences. Now Karen has 12 successful CDs, and she is booked nearly every weekend at functions that enliven her as well as her listeners. She currently earns more money as an independent musician than she did in the corporate world, and her soul is soaring, not cringing.

I cite the preceding examples to offer you a vision of how good your career can be if you are open to ease, flow, and creativity as ingredients for success. While the Hay House and Motek employees and Karen Drucker still face challenges and have their own learning curves of personal growth, their careers feel more like play than work. If that seems too good to be true, consider that such a career may be good enough to be true. Your old ceiling can become your new floor.

Labor of Love

Letting your life and career be easy does not mean that you get lazy, shirk responsibility, or lie in your bed and wait for checks to float through your window. You can be actively engaged in a passionate enterprise while holding a light heart. It may appear to others that you are working hard, but inwardly you are at one with your task and at peace with yourself.

When I wrote my first book, I was so immersed in the project that I wrote for 8, 12, and more hours each day and into the night. If you stood outside my door listening to me type, you might have thought, *That guy is really sweating it out.* But not so at all. I was enjoying every minute of the process. My sense of personal reward liberated immense energy to get the job done.

When you love what you do, what looks to others like work feels like play to you. When I am finished writing, teaching, or coaching, I have much more energy than when I began. I experience no struggle, because I am at peace with my vocation.

> Choose a job you love, and you'll never work another day in your life.
> — attributed to Confucius

"Right Livelihood," as Buddha called it, does not diminish your joy, but liberates it.

What to Sacrifice

If you must sacrifice something, sacrifice struggle. If you are going to give something up for Lent, give up suffering. If you are going to get sick, get

> I gladly make the "sacrifice" of fear.
> — *A Course in Miracles*

sick of living at less than full passion. If you are going to die, let your limited idea of self turn to dust.

Get over the idea that you must give up something you value for something you value more. Be clear on what you value most, and move wholeheartedly in that direction. When you stay true to your joy, loss is impossible. Loss is an illusion spun by the ego. In truth, we only grow in gain.

While you have been told that struggle is a fact of life, it is a belief to be grown beyond. Struggle was never God's will for us; those who say it is will one day receive a happy surprise. You end struggle by refusing to participate in it and valuing inner peace more. Sacrifice did not make the sun rise for the Maya, and neither will it buy you what you fear to lose. Today would be a great day to turn in your hardaholic badge and let life lay its gifts at your doorstep.

The important thing is this: To be able at any moment to sacrifice that which we are for what we could become.

— **Charles Du Bos**

16

DESPERATION
REPELS

*What we call our despair is often only the
painful eagerness of unfed hope.*

— GEORGE ELIOT

As Sandy approached age 40, she desperately wanted a husband and child. The closer she came to her birthday, the more anxious she felt, fearing she would soon be too old to be a mother. Sandy feverishly dated many men, most of whom were inappropriate and disappointing. Some created dramatic scenes that embarrassed her in public, leaving her frazzled and frustrated.

In coaching I explained to Sandy that when you identify yourself as desperate and you act out of desperation, you get desperate results. Desperation is the offspring of the marriage of fear and illusion, and nothing good can come of that unholy union. By virtue of the Law of Attraction, Sandy was not drawing unto herself quality candidates for a relationship and fatherhood. Instead, she attracted men as lost and confused as she was. If you enter a relationship in order to offset your emptiness, the relationship *exaggerates* your emptiness.

Over time I encouraged Sandy to relax about her need to have a husband and child by age 40, and trust that if such a situation were in her best interests, it would come about in a natural and organic way without her having to struggle to manufacture it. I also suggested that she date men because she enjoyed their company rather than running them through the gauntlet of potential "husbandry" and fatherhood.

Sandy accepted my advice and began to let go of her desperate attitude. She dated men she liked and approached her relationships from the here and now, rather than setting them up for a future goal.

I didn't hear from Sandy for quite a while, and then I received her wedding photo, followed a year later by her baby's photo. When Sandy moved from a position of desperation to trust, her heart's desire came to her.

More Like It

While it may seem that acting out of desperation will draw to you what you want, it actually repels it. When you say, feel, or live, "I do not and cannot have what I want, and I feel miserable because of it," you are affirming the absence of what you want and perpetuating that condition. Yet you can just as easily (actually far *more* easily) affirm the presence of your good and attract more of *that* to you.

The dynamics of desperation and confidence play out in couples who are trying to get pregnant but can't. They really, really want to have a baby; and they try all kinds of methods and treatments, some quite expensive, to do so. Still they fail to get pregnant. Each month when the woman realizes she has not conceived, the couple becomes more frustrated and disappointed, fearing they will not have the child they want so very much.

Eventually the couple gives up trying to conceive, and they adopt a child. Then, lo and behold, within a short time the woman becomes pregnant, and the couple has their own biological child.

When a couple feels desperate about not conceiving, their underlying belief and affirmation is: *We cannot have a baby. There is no baby. No baby, no baby, no baby.* Since the images and feelings we hold in our subconscious generate our experience, no baby shows up.

When the couple adopts a baby, their focus shifts from *No baby, no baby, no baby . . . and we are so disappointed,* to *Baby, baby, baby . . . and we are really happy!* At that point their subconscious beliefs and pictures have transformed dramatically. They are now on the "baby" wavelength, so that is what manifests.

Whether you want a partner, baby, career, or any other goal, if you can move from the *I need it, and I don't have it* frequency to the *I can and do have it* frequency, the Law of Attraction will assist you with the mechanics of manifestation.

More Shall Be Given

The Bible states a strange principle: "For whosoever hath, to him shall be given, and he shall have more abundance: but whosoever hath not, from him shall be taken away even that he hath" (Matthew 13:12). While at first glance this dynamic seems unfair, deeper examination reveals a key principle:

If you want to attract more of anything, affirm the attributes that correspond to your intention. When Karen Drucker began her music career, she did not have a lot of money. At the time she decided to subscribe to a music magazine. On the subscription form she found two boxes: one for *Regular Subscription* and another at a lower rate for *Starving Musician.* "I was tempted to check the *Starving Musician* box," Karen recounts. "But then I realized that in that act I would be affirming poverty and consequently manifest that in my experience. So I took a leap of faith, checked the *Regular Subscription* box, and made the payment at that rate. The next day I received several checks and invitations for gigs. My affirmation paid off immediately."

Confidence speaks louder than words. If you are selling something, your customer will be more impressed with your energy than your pitch. Your energy *is* your pitch.

While shopping for a new car, I went to a dealership where a salesperson swooped on me like a hungry vulture. His desperate energy was so annoying that I did not even take a car for a test-drive. At another dealership I was greeted by a relaxed, easygoing salesperson. I felt no hype from him, and when he invited me for a test-drive, I felt drawn to go with him.

During the drive the salesman said little, but noted the rich color of the surf on the beach we were passing. I commented on how nicely the car drove, and he simply agreed, letting the car sell itself. By the time we returned to the dealership, I had bought the car. His confidence in the quality of his product was more compelling to me than all the words he might have said in its favor. I might have purchased a car from the first dealership I visited as readily as the second one. Yet my experience of the salesperson's confidence was a strong factor in my choice.

Surveys indicate that the deeper a political candidate's voice, the more likely people are to vote for that candidate. A deep tone of voice generally indicates relaxation, a sign of confidence. On some level we are programmed to recognize confidence and be more attracted to it than desperation.

The One Justified Desperation

Since everything that exists has a purpose in some situation ("Even a clock that is stopped is right twice a day"), is the experience of desperation *ever* justified?

Indeed it is, in this way: If you get to a point on your path where you have severely distanced yourself from well-being, and you desperately want to reconnect with inner peace, such desperation motivates you to find healing. In that case, desperation serves as a powerful energizer to make a needed course correction.

Many people who find themselves in the throes of addiction, for example, come to a point where they intensely seek relief from their pain. I know a fellow who had been a longtime alcoholic until one day he woke up in a strange bed covered with his own vomit. "At that moment I realized I had strayed as far from a decent life as I possibly could. I knew I needed help." He went to Alcoholics Anonymous and turned his life around.

While most people believe they are desperate for a person, thing, or situation outside themselves, they are really desperate for self-love, a sense of empowerment, and the recognition of well-being in and around them. Desperation for inner peace is entirely different from desperation for an external result, since what you are seeking is within you, and you have access to it. You cannot be truly desperate for something you already own and deserve.

You can have everything you want, because you already own everything you need. When you recognize that love, joy, wisdom, peace, and power are within you, everything that matches those attributes will show up in your outer world as a reflection. Never define yourself as desperate or act desperately. Instead, define yourself as whole and worthy, and everything whole and worthy will be yours.

17

WHEN DO YOU
GET TO ENJOY IT?

The foolish man seeks happiness in the distance:
The wise grows it under his feet.

— JAMES OPPENHEIM

A number of years ago I found my work overwhelming, and I decided to take a sabbatical from my business. At the time I was being coached by a gifted intuitive counselor who supported me to slow down and take better care of myself.

A month into my sabbatical, I found myself still working at tasks I had planned to stop doing. A habit-driven voice inside me urged, *You must finish these projects and communications before you can relax.* As a result I found myself still chained to my desk and computer, feeling more frustrated than ever.

Around that time I had a session with my counselor. I told her, "I still feel overwhelmed with endless tasks."

She replied pointedly, "Have you ever thought about taking a sabbatical?

Bam! Right between the eyes. My counselor knew full well that I was supposed to be *on* a sabbatical. She was rubbing in the fact that I had not done what I intended to do. While her comment irritated me, it prodded me powerfully: *If you are going to take care of yourself, the only time to do it is now. No excuses.*

Motivated by her guidance, I pulled myself away from my self-created obligations and began to travel, spend time in nature, and enjoy my relationship with my partner. The remainder of the sabbatical was truly a sabbatical—but only when I *chose* it to be so.

Contentment never comes in the future, because the future is never here. Contentment comes only when you choose it *now.* If your good is always waiting for you around the corner, it will *always* be around the corner. If, however, you are willing to let your good be here now, you will find it here now, and when you come around the corner, you will find it here now again.

What you seek may already be in your hands, but you must look in your hands to find it. Happiness is like a winning lottery ticket. Having the ticket is not enough. If you intend to collect your earnings, you must go to the lottery office and say, "Here is my ticket. I want my money." Likewise, you must go to the universal lottery office and say, "Here is my birthright. I want my peace."

Tigers and Strawberries

A man was walking through a jungle when two tigers began to chase him. He ran to the edge of a cliff and began to shimmy down a vine into a canyon. As he approached the valley floor, he found two more tigers waiting for him. He looked up and saw a pair of mice gnawing at the vine on which he was suspended. Just then he noticed some succulent strawberries growing out of a nook on the side of the cliff. He reached out, plucked a handful, and ate them, smiling as he savored the sweetest strawberries he had ever tasted.

Sometimes it seems that there are tigers behind us, ahead of us, and all around us. Trouble appears to threaten at every turn, and prospects for escape seem dim. Yet if you shift your gaze from the apparent threat, you might find some delicious strawberries. When you make up your mind to stay in strawberry consciousness, you will rise above tiger consciousness, and strawberries will become the dominant theme of your reality.

My friend Victoria owned a gift shop that was often pilfered by shoplifters in her small town. One day she was robbed by two teenage boys who lifted more than $3,000 worth of merchandise. At that point Victoria grew frantic; it was easy to overlook a $5 ring, but now she had lost merchandise she hadn't even paid for.

Victoria called the police, who knew the boys—they were already on house arrest. She went to the house with the police, and the teenagers denied the theft. As Victoria looked into the eyes of one of the boys, she saw that his soul was aching. Compassion filled her heart, and she understood that these young men were calling for help. The robbery had occurred for a purpose deeper than appearances would indicate.

Victoria informed the district attorney that she wanted to raise money to enable these boys to attend the Landmark Forum, a transformational program. The DA agreed to support her even though the boys were incarcerated. Six more teenagers who wanted to participate in the program came forth, and Victoria phoned everyone she knew and spoke at her church in an attempt to raise money for the program. She collected more than $3,000 in a short period of time. A gracious woman offered her San Francisco home for a weekend seminar for eight teens and four adults, where significant shifts in attitude and behavior occurred.

Using that experience as a platform, Victoria founded a nonprofit organization through which many teenagers' lives were uplifted. Now she reports that she is grateful she was robbed; the experienced changed her life, along with those of many others. In the midst of tigers, she plucked the strawberries and ultimately fed the tigers as well as herself.

What They Serve in Heaven

The places where we seek fulfillment are often not where true fulfillment lives. The world tells us that stuff, power, and prestige will bring us joy; the more people you boss, the more important you are. Yet real joy is found in connection. The mind fragments, while the heart joins.

When Dee and I lived in Fiji, we frequented a restaurant called Oasis in the small town of Pacific Harbour. We dined there not just for the tasty food, but because we savored our connection with a native Fijian waitress named Litia. The night we met Litia, we felt as if we were reunited with a dear friend. She welcomed us with a huge smile, touched us as she seated us, called us "darling," and took impeccable care of us. At the time, Dee and I were considering purchasing a property in the area, and we decided to go ahead, in part because we so enjoyed the warmth of the Fijian people typified by Litia.

Over the years our relationship with Litia deepened, and our appreciation for her grew. She was kind and generous with all the patrons, and made the weariest travelers feel at home. On numerous occasions we observed tourists from more prosperous countries become demanding, rude, and even insulting toward Litia. They were fussy about special orders and substitutions, impatient for their meal, and treated her like a peon. In all cases Litia maintained her poise and returned their rudeness with extreme kindness.

I was stunned by the juxtaposition of power and peace in these encounters. Here were wealthy travelers who had the means to afford expensive vacations, obviously used to having "subservients" snap to their orders. Before them was a humble woman living in one of the poorest countries in the world, who earned a minimal salary (no tips) and used all of her income to help her children. Yet she was far happier than the well-to-do tourists. Through those interactions I learned that happiness has nothing to do with worldly power and everything to do with inner light. This modest waitress was far closer to heaven than those making demands of her.

Litia consistently demonstrated that inner peace is the greatest power. All the prestige in the world does not light the universe as brightly as the glow of a sincere heart.

Beyond Surviving . . . into Thriving

My friend Tony went through cancer treatment and emerged healthy. He told me that he does not attend a cancer-survivor support group. He attends a group for *thrivers*. "There is more to life than simply surviving," Tony told me. "I am here to shine."

There is a huge difference between surviving and thriving. When I think of surviving, I think of the television series *Survivor*, in which individuals with separate interests are pitted against each other, competing to see who will triumph over the losers. It is a primal mentality, and a scanty substitute for real happiness.

Thriving, on the other hand, conjures far more empowering images. I think of the school that Oprah Winfrey established in Africa so children can gain skills for a healthy, rewarding, productive life. I think of companies such as Apple, Microsoft, Google, Facebook, eBay, Netflix, and Groupon coming up with clever, colorful, and creative ways to enhance modern commerce, communication, and entertainment. I think of theaters filled with patrons enjoying concerts, plays, movies, lectures, and gatherings that stimulate our higher senses and bring us laughter, music, dance, and wisdom.

The Eastern system of chakras, or energy centers in the body, reflects a profoundly designed ladder of well-being. The first chakra, located at the base of the spine, is concerned only with survival needs. At the top of the head the seventh chakra mediates our oneness with the universe and finds fulfillment in our spiritual nature. While all of the chakras are functioning all the time, we decide which rung of the ladder we choose to stand upon. The journey from the lower chakras to the higher ones is the map of human evolution.

Although most people in our culture have everything we need to survive, and we are fully capable of dwelling in a state of self-actualization, for some odd reason we tend to gravitate toward struggling at a survival level. Yet, like my friend Tony, you can re-

> The glory of God is humanity fully alive.
> — St. Irenaeus

fuse to settle for an identity as a survivor and instead see yourself as a thriver. You may already be sitting at the top of the pyramid of life, but missing the view. In the Old Testament (Genesis 13:14), God told Abram (later Abraham), "Now lift up your eyes and look from the place where you are, northward and southward and eastward and westward." The instruction was more metaphorical than literal: Raise your vision from the small and demeaning to the expansive and celebratory. There is a far greater world available to you than the one you have been living in.

Happiness Envy

In the film *Broadcast News,* a neophyte reporter who is intensely happy asks a veteran newsman what to do when your real life exceeds your dreams. The elder tells the fellow to just keep it to himself.

The oddest effect of happiness is that other people are often annoyed by it. Misery *does* love company, so a joyful person poses a threat to those steeped in sorrow. This is so for a couple of reasons:

— First, people who perceive a reward for being lost, sick, alone, poor, or victimized have an investment in their reality. When someone comes along who challenges that reality, teeth are bared in an effort to get rid of the intruder bringing sunshine to a rainy but familiar *perceived* safe domain.

— Second, observing a happy person stimulates the psychodynamic of envy. If I want something but haven't been able to get it, and I see that you have it, your success reminds me of what I am missing. So you become the bad guy for underscoring my pain.

One way I can level the playing field is to try to tear you down so we are both groveling.

If these responses to happiness sound sick, irrational, foolish, immature, and self-destructive, they are. But hey, the ego has never been known for its kindness and love to self and others. Shining the spotlight on its trickery is the beginning of loosening its hold and replacing it with thoughts, feelings, and actions that truly serve.

When you choose contentment, happiness, or any other form of positive self-expression, you are likely to encounter people who mistrust, challenge, criticize, and ridicule you. I remember walking into an office, smiling. Upon seeing me, the secretary snarled, "And what the hell are *you* so happy about?"

What do you do with people who can't handle your happiness? Don't let them steal it from you. Hold your space and remember that well-being is far more natural than resistance to it. Don't take the negativity of others personally, don't argue with them, don't try to prove anything, and don't flaunt your glee. Just live it. Regard their envy as a compliment, an indication that your light is obvious. While others may try to tear you down, they do not have the power to do so unless you give it to them. You are connected to a Higher Power, and they are disconnected. Although they realize it not, your peace is a gift to them. On some level you are inspiring them. Later they will join you.

If you feel envious of someone who is happier than you are, reframe the experience in your favor. Everyone you observe is a reflection of your own consciousness. If you are aware of the happiness or success of others, something inside you is already a match to their state of being. They are mirroring an

> You spot it, you got it.
> — Source unknown

element of yourself that is emerging. It is only a matter of time, perhaps a short time, until the good you observe in their lives will become your own. Appreciate such people as role models and harbingers of the success that you deserve and will manifest.

The world is a smorgasbord of possible realities, and you get to live in the one defined by the vision you choose. All vision is selective. Every encounter, experience, and event is testimony to the vision you are putting into service.

We see more with our minds than with our eyes. If the mind is steeped in judgments and shrouded by fear, the world it shows us bears little resemblance to what life could be if we let it. We must retrain our vision to see with the inner spiritual eye.

When do you get to enjoy your life? Now, if you choose it.

It is only with the heart that one can see rightly.
What is essential is invisible to the eye.

— **ANTOINE DE SAINT-EXUPÉRY,** FROM *THE LITTLE PRINCE*

18

God Did Not Leave You

Keep your faith in all beautiful things.
In the sun when it is hidden. . . . In the spring when it is gone.

— Roy R. Gilson

"I was married for ten years to an emotionally abusive man," a caller named Jackie shared on my program, *Get Real,* on Hay House Radio. "He controlled every aspect of my life, from how I wore my hair, to the friends I could associate with, to when and how we had sex. I was miserable, but I just accepted this as a requirement of my marriage. I was afraid he would leave me if I didn't cooperate.

"Finally I admitted to myself how unhappy I was. Tearfully I phoned my friend Lindsay, who told me that no one should accept the kind of tyranny I was experiencing. She gave me the name of a counselor, and over time I gained the confidence to leave that marriage. Now I am angry at God for leaving me in that bad situation for so long."

I told Jackie, "God didn't leave you in that situation. You chose to stay. God was the one who told you to phone Lindsay."

We have all done things we regret and allowed other people to do things to us that we regret. Afterward we may feel betrayed, used, or resentful. We might hold a grievance against others or continue to beat ourselves up for being naïve or stupid. We may lose faith in people, God, or life.

Three facts of life: (1) we all make mistakes, (2) the experiences we call mistakes offered us benefits at the time, and (3) the lessons we learn from the mistakes and the growth we gain far outshine any temporary losses.

Your universal support system is far greater than your errors or the people who let you down. People may betray or desert you, but the potential for love is always with you. For every mistake you make, or someone makes against you, there is a way to offset, remedy, or heal it.

Free will gives us the power to stay in painful situations, and it also gives us the power to leave or transform them, and to learn through them.

You have your idea about how your life is supposed to go, or who is supposed to be there for you, when, and how . . . but life has a bigger idea. In the aftermath of a disappointing experience, you may experience a huge growth spurt that the event facilitated.

> Disappointment is the hook upon which God hangs His victories.
> — Source unknown

Or someone who really cares might show up, which leads to a richer friendship than the one you lost. Or you might discover an unexpected avenue that takes you where you need to go, a pathway you never would have found if you stayed in your old routine. Sometimes the greatest good comes from what at the time seemed like the densest bad.

If you rigidly cling to your notion of how you should be helped, you are limiting the channels through which your good can reach you. Regret and resentment spew a psychic smoke screen that clouds your ability to see clearly or act effectively. Biologists tell us that when you are upset, your peripheral vision narrows to tunnel vision. From a survival standpoint, this makes perfect sense. If you are a deer fleeing from a lion, you don't have time to enjoy the scenery. You must fixate intensely on finding a safe haven.

The same process occurs psychologically when you feel threatened. In a state of fear you see few options (or none), while there may be many. Mental health may be gauged by the number of options you are aware are available to you. If you are seeing many options, you are probably relaxed, clear, and in a positive frame of mind. If you see few or no options, you are probably upset and not in a good position to make healthy choices. This is why it is unwise to make important decisions when you are upset. If possible, wait until you are relaxed and in a clearer state of mind. Then you will see more options and recognize those that will serve you best.

Avenues and Source

In medieval times, tall buildings were adorned with statue heads of gargoyles at the corners of their roofs. Rainwater fell onto the roof, into gutters, and poured out of the gargoyles' mouths. If you were looking up from the street and did not know better, you might think that the gargoyles were producing the rain. But they were not. The rain was coming from the heavens, and the statues' mouths were the last channel through which the water flowed before it reached Earth.

Likewise, you may believe that a particular person, home, or job is the source of your good. But such entities are simply gargoyles through which a far greater source flows. If one of the gargoyles is blocked, there are many other mouths through which the rain may issue. Do not confuse the avenue with the source. The source of your good is infinite universal supply. While individual delivery persons may falter or disappear, your ultimate source is utterly dependable.

Better Off Anyway

Sometimes if no one helps you, the message is that you do not need help from another person. You might gain more by reaching inside yourself to figure something out. The insight you gain empowers you in ways more beneficial than if someone else gave you the answer or rescued you. Or you may discover that you did not need help at all, or the change you sought to make was unnecessary. Or events took you in a better direction than if your specified helper had come through. If you need help, you will get it. If you don't, you will receive a different kind of benefit.

My friend Jenny married a fellow who had three teenage sons from a previous marriage. Their mother's family was quite wealthy, so they lived on trust funds. The boys never worked, cleaned, or did anything for themselves. Jenny was not about to be their servant, and she wanted to empower the boys to be independent and responsible for their lives. She taught them to cook, do their laundry, and clean the toilets. At first they scoffed and resisted, but soon they enjoyed mastering their tasks. When the boys grew up, one became a professional chef, and another owns and manages a vineyard. To this day they thank Jenny for helping them to help themselves.

Resentment, betrayal, or a sense of wasted time are interpretations. You can just as easily (*more* easily!) interpret such experiences in your favor. You can be deserted only at the shallowest level of observation. At a deeper and more substantial level, you have all the resources you need to master any task or overcome any challenge. You betray yourself by dwelling on thoughts of betrayal, and you empower yourself by dwelling on thoughts of support. People and experiences come and go, but love lives inside you. Go to where the love lives and you will never be abandoned.

19

LESS FIXING, MORE SAVORING

As each day comes to us refreshed and anew, so does my gratitude renew itself daily. The breaking of the sun over the horizon is my grateful heart dawning upon a blessed world.

— ATTRIBUTED TO **TERRI GUILLEMETS**

My friends Tim and Stacey bought a second home on St. John in the Virgin Islands. I remember sitting with them on the deck of their villa overlooking a sparkling white-sand beach kissed by soft azure waves. The ambient sunset glowed with colors that seemed beyond this world.

The couple planned to spend most of their time on the island, perhaps reside there full-time. But after living on St. John for six months, they returned to Philadelphia. Now they visit their tropical home twice a year for a few days each time. When I asked Tim and Stacey why they don't take advantage of their retreat more, they told me, "When we are there, we look around our property and all we see are projects. We can't really enjoy ourselves."

Just down the beach from Tim and Stacey's place lives a native family whose house has been in the family for generations. They, too, have projects, but they spend most of their time playing with their kids, walking on the beach, fishing, and barbecuing with friends. Their hacienda is not as modern or stylish as their neighbors'; the roof needs patching, the siding is aching for a paint job, and weeds practically eclipse the lawn. But the local family doesn't mind that much. They are too busy enjoying the place to worry about it.

Many of us have developed a habit of seeing what needs to be fixed rather than appreciating what is working. When we look at a person or thing, our minds immediately go to what's wrong and what needs to be changed. While improving ourselves and the world is a noble intention, if we get so caught up in fixing that we lose our ability to enjoy, work becomes our master rather than our servant. When obligations overshadow inspiration, we need to stop and revisit our priorities.

I used to own a lovely little cottage at the edge of a lake in the mountains, a perfectly idyllic setting. I would go there on weekends to rest, write, meditate, and putter with the landscaping.

One weekend my friend Stan came for a visit. Stan is a very busy guy involved in lots of projects. The moment he arrived, he began to make suggestions on how to improve the property: "You can pop out the wall of the cabin and add an extra bedroom" . . . "If you divert the driveway, you will have a straighter shot to the parking area" . . . "You could put a small turbine in the stream and get some electricity out of it."

While Stan meant well and his ideas were potentially good, the notion of turning the property into a project felt abrasive to me. I didn't buy the place to develop it. I bought it to enjoy it. When Stan finally left, I breathed a sigh of relief. Perhaps he came to remind me that some things are better enjoyed than developed.

From Self-Improvement to Self-Satisfaction

Many of us have undergone some kind of therapy or self-improvement program. Such endeavors are worthwhile only if we feel better about ourselves when we are done. Many forms of therapy or self-help do not improve our self-image, but keep us stuck in a vicious cycle of analyzing what's wrong. Woody Allen noted, "When I first went into psychotherapy I feared that I would emerge with the personality of a nineteenth-century neurotic Viennese cigar-smoking Jewish cocaine addict. . . . Now, after ten years in therapy, I would gladly have settled for that." I met a woman who had undergone seven years of primal-scream therapy. When she told her therapist that she felt a lot better and she was ready to leave therapy, he told her, "You are only just beginning." Does your therapy self-reinforce, or does it liberate?

You might also be fixated on fixing yourself physically. You might believe that you will become attractive once you lose ten pounds, emerge from the tanning salon brown as a berry, or fill out your bra more substantially. While such upgrades can make you feel better, will you feel satisfied and complete once they are done?

> If something is wrong, fix it if you can. But train yourself not to worry. Worry never fixes anything.
> — Mary Hemingway, quoting her neighbor Ole Helgerson

Probably not. When you perceive inadequacy in yourself, it is rarely offset by more fixing. Inadequacy is more effectively offset by deeper self-acceptance. It is not the objects of inadequacy that bug you, but the *perception* of inadequacy. If you perceive a problem with your body, the place to start fixing it is at its source—your thoughts about it—rather than at the level of their expression. Go ahead and make any improvements you prefer. Just don't use them as substitutes for self-love. There *is no* substitute for self-love.

Your "Get Out of Jail Free" Card

It's tempting to want to fix others and tell them how to live. But you have no idea how someone else should live. It's hard enough to figure out how *you* should live—so how could you even begin to know someone else's right path?

Help others if you can, but don't try to fix them. There is a big difference between helping and meddling. No one likes to be bugged, bossed, or altered to suit your purposes; they want to be loved and supported, not pushed. When tempted to help someone, meditate on *What would be truly helpful here?*

My mentor Hilda Charlton advised, "Before you tell your neighbor to pluck the weeds from her garden, be sure you have plucked the weeds from your own garden." She instructed each of us in the class to point a finger at someone else in the room. Then she asked us to notice how many fingers we had pointing at ourselves. The answer is *three*—each on our own hand.

When you point a finger at someone else, you have three pointing at yourself. Whenever you judge another person, you have already judged yourself, usually for the same perceived deficit. If you want to change the world, begin with yourself. When you are clear on your own path, you are in a far better position to help others get clear on theirs.

Hilda also taught us a mantra to use when we feel tempted to tell someone else how to live: *Not my business.* I used to have judgments about a chiropractor in my community who, in my opinion, had gotten caught up in a numbers and money game. While at the outset of his practice he seemed genuinely interested in helping people, over time his focus shifted more and more to simply increasing his volume of patients and his income. I grumbled to myself about this doctor and occasionally criticized him when I spoke to others. Then one day I realized that my adverse opinion affected him not in the least, and me in the most. So I decided to give him permission to live and breathe and practice as he was. Of course, he did not need my permission, for God had already granted that to him. *I* was the one who needed to be liberated.

A Course in Miracles tells us that when you keep someone else in a prison of your judgments about them, you have to stay in prison with them to be sure they don't escape. You must sit at the door of their cell to guard them. So you are just as much in prison as the person you are incarcerating—actually, more so if they don't share your judgments about them. Let other people out of the jail of your criticism, and you will be free, too.

Gorilla in Your Midst

The principle of *inattentional blindness* is dramatically demonstrated in an experiment captured on video by psychologists Daniel Simons and Christopher Chabris. In the 30-second clip, two small teams of college students, one wearing white T-shirts and the other wearing black T-shirts, are each passing a basketball to their own teammates. When I show this video in my seminars, I ask the audience to count the number of passes the white T-shirt team makes. To increase motivation, I offer a prize to the person who counts the correct number.

During the basketball session on video, someone wearing a gorilla suit walks into the midst of both teams. He stops, faces the camera, pounds his chest several times, and then exits. After the audience has watched the video, I ask them if anyone saw anything unusual. Amazingly, only about 25 percent of the people in the audience report that they saw the gorilla. Most of the viewers were so focused on counting the basketball passes that they did not see something that would otherwise be extremely obvious. When I replay the video, people are astonished to see the gorilla in their midst.

The dynamic of inattentional blindness plays out in many ways, two of which I will highlight: First, you can be so focused on what is not working or needs fixing that you completely overlook what *is* working and serving you. By the same token, you can be so focused on what is working and serving you that you are oblivious to what is *not* working.

While both of these principles are worth noting, let us here focus on the power of savoring our good so profoundly that the negative elements of our lives fade to the background and virtually disappear.

At this point you might argue, "Well, that's denial. If you turn your head from the bad in life, you're not being realistic." Understood. Yes, it's often necessary to address what is not working so you can fix it. Yet if you focus primarily on what is wrong, your mind becomes saturated in error, and you cloud your vision of pathways to effective change. What we call "reality" is quite subjective, a projection of the thoughts through which we filter our experience. The first step to world change is to cleanse "the doors of perception," as William Blake and Aldous Huxley suggested, rather than setting out on an endless quest to fix what is broken more in your mind than in reality.

If you are worried that savoring your life more will turn you into a blob and you will never grow or improve, take heart. If anything turns you into a blob that keeps you from growing and improving, it is fixation on fixing. Worry is the antithesis of improvement. Focusing on *solution* is the essence of improvement. Gratitude for *what is* provides the strongest platform for expanding into *what could be*. The more you find that is broken, the more you find that is broken. The more you find that is working, the more you find ways to make what is broken work.

Is This a Listen, or a Fix?

My friend Ted uses a brilliant technique when his wife tells him about a problem. After a few minutes of listening, he asks her, "Is this a *listen*, or is it a *fix?*" Are you telling me about this mainly to express yourself, or is there something you would like me to do?

Some things require fixing; others simply require a listen. If you automatically go into fix mode (generally a guy thing), you do not recognize your option to simply listen, and you will waste your energy. When I was in graduate school, my roommate told me about a problem he was having with his girlfriend. I immediately started to give him suggestions for resolving his issue. He told me, "I appreciate you trying to help, but you don't always have to have an answer. Sometimes I just need to get something off my chest or hear what I am saying. Then I can figure it out for myself."

If you tend to be a fixer, experiment with just listening— a lost art in our culture. Most people do not have conversations; they have parallel monologues. When others speak to you, are you with them, absorbing what they are saying and seeking to understand their viewpoint? Or are you busy thinking about the next thing you are going to say? You might be amazed by how much more fun it is to actually listen to someone rather than to be preparing your response. This is what real conversations are made of.

Life Beyond Fixing

Do you thrive on friends and clients calling you with their dramas so you can tell them what to do? Can you let others have their issues and problems and figure them out for themselves without rescuing them? If you had no one to fix or save, would you have a purpose in life?

If you have developed an identity as a fixer, your self-image may be confining you. People become compulsive fixers because: (1) fixing others removes the spotlight from their own problems; (2) they seek to fix themselves, and fixing others is a vicarious way of getting there; or (3) they feel important when others depend on them—they need to be needed.

While helping others is a great service, and on some level we all need to be needed, if you build your world around saving others, you miss broader possibilities for relationship. You also keep others small by identifying them as problematic or needy. What you do to others you automatically do to yourself, so you inherit the emptiness you ascribe to them. Helping is a gift, but creating dependency is damaging.

When you put aside the need to fix, you open the door to finding. You can relax and let life take care of itself without your needing to step in and save the day. If you need to help someone, you will know it and you will do it. But you will also have the option to allow others to carve their unique path, rather than turning every statement of upset into a rescue attempt.

The *Isness* Business

While standing in line at the motor-vehicle office, I noticed a fellow in front of me with his little boy at his side. I overheard the father say to someone, "My son is three years old. The doctor says he's too short for his age."

I wondered how that statement affected the child. Would this be the beginning of a lifetime of perceived inadequacy? Would he forever feel "less-than" about something he could not change? I looked at the child. To me he seemed a fairly normal height for a three-year-old. His problem was not his height; his problem was the chart the doctor consulted. The kid did not match someone else's idea of how tall he should be, so now he had a problem.

When I studied to become a human-relations trainer, I was taught to give people feedback only on things they could change. When you tell me, "Your eyes are too far apart," or "I wish you were more like your brother," that feedback is not helpful, because you are noting attributes that I cannot or would not change. When you tell a little boy, "You are too short," you are setting him up for frustration and low self-esteem. When you tell him, "I love you no matter what height you are," you set him up to win at life.

At a dinner party Dee and I hosted, my friend Denise reported that she had just come from seeing a psychic healer, who told her that her chakras were out of balance and her body was filled with parasites. This led to a lengthy discussion among the guests, including lots of advice for Denise about how to regain her health. She was also dealing with a weight issue, which elicited numerous recommendations from the group.

As I listened, I was uncomfortable with the general tone of the conversation, which went something like: "There is plenty wrong with you, and we are going to tell you how to fix it." When Denise stepped away from the group, I took her aside and told her, "I love you just the way you are. I know there are things you are working on, but right now I find you perfect, and I appreciate all you are and all you do for me and others."

Tears welled up in my friend's eyes as she told me, "Thank you. After that barrage of advice, that's just what I needed to hear."

I was not suggesting to Denise that she overlook any conditions that were causing her pain, or that she should not make an effort to improve her health and feel better. I was simply affirming Denise's beauty and worth right where she stood on her healing journey.

You and I also walk a healing journey. We progress toward wellness more when we proceed *from* wellness than when we *seek* it.

The real you does not need fixing. Only the surface layer of you seems to need improvement. Your innate wholeness has never been damaged except in your thoughts. You have been taught that life is a problem, you are defective, and you must face and overcome an endless series of issues and obstacles before you can be enough. None of that is true. Your perfection is unsullied, and your brokenness is illusion. You are not a black hole that needs to be filled. You are a light that needs to be shined. Less fixing, more savoring. Your inner self already owns a glorious beach house. How much time you spend there is up to you.

20

EXECUTING THE MISSIONARY POSITION

Men will wrangle for religion; write for it;
fight for it; die for it; anything but _live_ for it.

— CHARLES CALEB COLTON

A friend of mine was getting a massage when the massage therapist asked her if she had been saved. Oh dear . . .

We have all been confronted by people who want to convert us to their religion, multilevel-marketing company, or belief system. Perhaps you have attempted to convert others. Such interactions can be stimulating if you are up for a theological discussion or attracted to a product. But many people find them annoying. When young men in black pants and white short-sleeve shirts approach my yard, I inform them that I am the gardener and Mr. Cohen has moved to Fiji. When they depart, I thank God that I have been saved.

The Guinness Book of World Records cites the longest conversation in recorded history as transpiring between a Jehovah's Witness and an Amway salesman. I respect religious devotees and multilevel-marketing aficionados for their faith and determination. They believe in their pathway or product, and want to share the benefits they have discovered. Yet why do so many people run the other way when others try to sell them God or soap powder?

Proselytizing is motivated by insecurity. People who do not have confidence in themselves, their God, or their product need to amass legions of believers around them to compensate for their perceived emptiness. The more people you need to get to agree with you, the less you trust your own knowing.

An inspired invitation to participate, on the other hand, proceeds from inner security. Confident belief is content to simply express itself, is unattached to results, and trusts that those who can benefit will recognize truth and be uplifted. It is less important that you join my religion, and more important that we are joined with each other. Faith acknowledges many routes to the mountaintop and respects all paths as valid. Fear shouts, "My way is the only way!" and seeks to meet the needs of the converter more than the converted. Many have been killed in the name of dogma. Many more have been healed by unconditional love.

> First you talk the talk.
> Then you talk the walk.
> Then you walk the talk.
> Then you walk the walk.
> — Source unknown

People founded in faith motivate others by example. When you model the behavior you wish to inculcate, your message is far more compelling than when you resort to histrionics, games, gimmicks, and threats.

The less you believe, the more you need to convince. The more you believe, the less you need to say. Authentic sales or conversion occurs more at an energetic level than a

> Never buy hair grower from a bald salesman.
> — Source unknown

verbal level. Everyone is unconsciously reading your energy more than your words. *Be* the life you wish the world would live.

How to Change the Whole World

The desire to get everyone to do what you do cloaks your desire to experience more of what you value. I met a fellow who practices *watsu,* a delightfully soothing method of massage in body-temperature water. He told me, "My goal is for everyone in the world to get a watsu treatment."

While worldwide watsu would probably make the planet a better place, his vision was not realistic or even necessary. Not everybody in the world will ever get a watsu treatment, not everybody wants one, and not everyone needs one. The fellow's intention was benign, yet inherently a projection of his own value system. What he really meant was: "I feel so wonderful when I receive watsu that I want my entire world to be filled with that good feeling." The operative words here are *"the* world" and *"my* world." If he could just recognize that his mission in life was to elevate his *own* consciousness, he could leave the other seven billion people on the planet to discover their unique healing paths, and he would reach his goal far more quickly and easily.

In the movie *The Karate Kid* (2010 version), the student begins to sense the power of his martial-arts practice. He tells the master that he would like to control lots of other people with this power. The master shakes his head and tells the student that there is only one person he needs to control—himself. All of our efforts to gain mastery over others are but veiled distractions from the challenge of mastering our own selves . . . the only real mastery required and of which we are capable.

Trying to convince others to do what you do is generally ego motivated and counterproductive. Real conversion or uplifting of others occurs only when love, not fear, is at the root of the experience. The root word of *religion* means "to join together," as with a Higher Power. When you are connected with your Higher Power, the light you radiate stimulates those who look upon you to connect with *their* Higher Power—ultimately the same as yours—and far beyond any particular religion or human pathway.

Finding God never has anything to do with the promise of future heaven or the threat of future hell. God is realized only now, for heaven is a state of mind available right where you stand. Eternity does not start after you die; it begins when you really live. Those who threaten you with the flames of Hades are already there. The fear of death *is* death, and the threat of hell *is* hell.

If you are happy with your religion, spiritual path, product, or life, others will be drawn to follow in your footsteps—not because they fear going to hell if they don't, but because they will find a touch of heaven if they do. Alcoholics Anonymous and other 12-step programs are built upon a mature tenet: "We rely on attraction, not promotion." They suggest and invite, but do not coerce. Those who come to 12-step programs do so because they recognize the value of the system. They are free to come and go as they please, and most stay because they want to, not because they will be punished if they don't.

> My religion is very simple.
> My religion is kindness.
> — His Holiness the Dalai Lama

Is God love, or fear? When you get clear on this answer, all the other questions in your life will answer themselves. The sage Meher Baba put it most eloquently:

> Love has to spring spontaneously from within; it is in no way amenable to any form of inner or outer force. Love and co-ercion can never go together; but while love cannot be forced upon anyone, it can be awakened through love itself. Love is essentially self-communicative; those who do not have it catch it from those who have it. Those who receive love from others cannot be its recipients without giving a response that, in itself, is the nature of love. True love is unconquerable and irresistible. It goes on gathering power and spreading itself until eventually it transforms everyone it touches. Humanity will attain a new mode of being and life through the free and unhampered interplay of pure love from heart to heart.

The Law of Allowing

The Teachings of Abraham (Abraham-Hicks) delineate three basic universal laws: the *Law of Attraction,* the *Law of Deliberate Creation,* and the *Law of Allowing.* The Law of Allowing states that each of us must follow our own unique path in life, and we must allow others to follow theirs.

You do not have the right or power to choose for another person because: (1) from your limited perspective, you cannot know what is right for them; and (2) if you impose your choice on them, you rob them of important lessons they can learn only by walking through them personally. To try to manipulate another person to do as you wish is not just selfish, but fruitless. If you have ever tried to get your spouse to change to live up to your expectations, your efforts likely failed and caused more problems than they solved. Certainly you may invite, suggest, support, and offer help or guidance where you can, but ultimately the choice to accept your offering is in the hands of the recipient.

The Law of Allowing calls you to trust that other people are capable of succeeding without your managing their lives. This applies most obviously to parenting and teaching. When my friend Jenny's stepsons (described in a previous chapter) got into jams, she struggled to

> A happy outcome to all things is sure.
> — *A Course in Miracles*

get them out. Yet over time she realized that the boys gained more by learning the lessons the jams provided. Eventually she came up with a mantra that has helped her and her kids time and again: *They'll figure it out.* Now Jenny helps where she can through word, action, and prayer. But beyond that, she trusts the process of learning and empowers her kids by regarding them as wise and resourceful.

Exit Doors That Work

One way to evaluate any religion, self-development path, or organization is to observe whether it has an exit door or graduation mechanism. Many pathways have subtle or obvious rules or pressure tactics to keep members in the fold. If you declare that you are ready to move on, the institution goes into intense threat-and-survival mode. Leaders tell you that you need to stay in the organization for life or you will be lost or go to hell.

It is a rare organization or leader that can say, "Thank you for joining us for the time you did. We now trust your decision to move on, and we wish you well." Instead, when you tell such an organization you are leaving, or you leave without telling them, the group calls in its heavies and does everything in its power to force you to stay. Some religions practice shunning and treat you like a criminal or a nobody if you start to stray. Other cults will hound you for years with letters, phone calls, visits, and threats. If you want to assess the level of health of an organization, study how it deals with those who leave.

You can gauge your sense of enoughness by your attitude surrounding leaving an organization or relationship. Do you feel guilty and avoid communicating about your departure? Do you offer excuses, leave abruptly, create a drama, or make the organization or person you are leaving "wrong"? Do you feel like a failure or judge your tenure with the group or person as a mistake or waste of time? Or can you stand tall in dignity and integrity, thank the group or person for the time and lessons you shared, and firmly declare with love, "It's time for me to move on."

People who join cults or religions because they believe they are not enough are an energetic match to the organization when they join. Populated by people who feel they are not enough, the organization has a sense of non-enoughness built into its fiber, so it attracts or preys upon people who believe *they* are not enough.

When you grow beyond your sense of inadequacy, you have graduated from the belief that moved you to join, and the agreement of *not enough* no longer binds you and the group together. So you must move on to find and bond with other people or groups based on an agreement of adequacy.

This is not to say that religions or cultlike groups do not help people. They do. If you are steeped in an addiction, fear, pain, or a dysfunctional lifestyle, and you find a belief system that uplifts you and brings you healing and a more fulfilling life, the religion or group serves well. Many lives are improved by participating in groups that are not fully healthy. All cults are based on at least a seed of truth that attracts people to join. If you cultivate that seed, you gain for life. Yet if that seed is accompanied by myriad illusions or oppressive dogma, you cannot afford to stay.

Often there is a period of transition between leaving a group or relationship based on *not enough* and connecting with people and groups based on *enough*. This can be a confusing or frightening period in which you feel lost, alone, or abandoned. You might be tempted to return to the group or relationship for a sense of familiarity and security. But the genie is out of the bottle, and you can no longer stuff him or her into a container that has been outgrown.

> Resolve to evolve.
> — Source unknown

When the newly liberated Hebrew nation left slavery and found itself in the wilderness, some of the people cried out, "Let's go back to Egypt! We were slaves there, but at least we had food, shelter, and security." Some did return, as did some African-American slaves who did not know how to deal with their freedom when it was granted. Yet most of the Hebrews and African Americans realized that the challenges of freedom were more attractive than the "security" of slavery, so they forged on to claim the gifts of independence.

Those gifts are available to you when you mobilize the trust and courage to keep moving ahead. Healthy partners or groups will support you in your decision to grow, and even celebrate with you. Be grateful for those who rejoice in your freedom. There *are* healthy ways to leave, and if you choose that path, your learning is further fortified.

There are two ways that participating in a relationship, religion, or organization empowers you: first, when you enter with a whole heart; and second, when you leave with a whole heart. The hidden gift of a conscious departure is that, in a sense, you are not really going anywhere. Where there is love and caring, the relationship is forever. You are not leaving the love, just the form that the love has taken. You can remain friends and mutual supporters for a lifetime, a hallmark of enoughness that pays a compliment both to you and the group or relationship from which you are moving on.

Everything Serves

If you've participated in a religion or cult that has misled or abused you, you may be tempted to blame the organization or become soured on God or self-improvement groups. Yet blame and resentment only perpetuate pain and keep the negative experience alive in your psyche. Consider, instead, that you are not the victim of the group, but rather value the gifts you gleaned from the experience. They include:

- The truth principles you learned via the group's philosophy

- The healing and life enhancement you gained by putting those principles into action

- The relationships and fellowship you enjoyed

- The growth you sustained by taking your power back after you had given it away, and departing by conscious choice

Ultimately the experience of participating in the group served you on many levels. *All* experiences in life are either to be enjoyed or learned from. Your relationship with the group or person provided you both.

> It all ends up in the good pile.
> — Mike Grefner

There was a reason and purpose for you to join the group when you did, and a reason and purpose for you to leave when you did. Now there is a reason and purpose for you

> The inconvenience is temporary.
> The improvement is permanent.
> Thank you for your patience.
> — Sign in a highway construction zone

to move on and connect with others who are a match to the frequency at which you are living or wish to live. Evolution is proceeding wisely.

When you know that you are enough, you don't need anyone to agree with you, join you, or prove your adequacy. Your worth cannot be bestowed by a group or by surrounding yourself with a posse. Your value is intrinsic, not earned. It is internally hardwired, not imported. You do not need to proselytize or be proselytized, because the Law of Attraction guides everyone to be in their right place without pressure or struggle.

When religions, self-development groups, and sales forces honor innate wisdom and wholeness, there will be no need for membership campaigns. How could you join the elite group created in the image and likeness of God when you are already a lifetime member?

21

FIRE THE
IN-BETWEENERS

...but while I breathe Heaven's air, and Heaven looks down on me...
I remain Mistress of mine own self and mine own soul.

— ALFRED, LORD TENNYSON

My business manager Marty was a real go-getter. He loved to work the corporate system in his favor, and he usually succeeded. When we moved our office to a rural location in Hawaii, Marty asked the telephone company to install several lines in our new building. To his chagrin, he was told that due to the archaic phone system in the area, we would be able to get only one line. This did not work for our company, since we needed at least two lines for our various business activities.

Marty pursued the project as he usually did, by working his way "up the food chain" of the telephone company. Eventually he entered into a dialogue with the company's state director of consumer services, who gave him the same dismal report. Deflated, Marty came to me and reported that even the highest power in the telephone company could not help him.

I thought about the situation and suggested, "There's a Power higher than the director you spoke to. Let's appeal to that Power." I invited Marty to join me in holding the situation in prayer and trust in the help of divine order—which we did.

The day of the telephone installation came, and a service technician showed up at the door of our new office. We explained our situation to him, and he told us he would check the local wiring system. After running a few tests, he reported, "No problem. I can put in your two lines." By the end of the afternoon, we had both lines working. Apparently there was a Director who superseded the director of consumer services.

While religions and other spiritual teachings have told you that you need to go through various saints, deities, masters, and gurus to get to God, you can go direct if you choose.

> Guru, God, and self are one.
> — Ramana Maharshi

In the early stages of your spiritual journey, you can benefit by summoning the aid of entities you perceive to be outside yourself. Ultimately, you need to claim the presence and power of the divinity

> Who looks outside, dreams.
> Who looks inside, awakens.
> — attributed to Carl Jung

within yourself. Who or what lives outside you, lives inside you. The entities you worshipped or summoned represent aspects of your own consciousness.

The source of creation does not live on a distant cloud or in a faraway galaxy. It lives in and through you, as well as in the heavenly cosmos. You will find no more of it elsewhere. Everything you seek is where you stand.

Beyond Hierarchy

If you have gone to church, served in the military, worked in the corporate world, or eaten in a high-school cafeteria, you are well aware of a system of ranks. Top dogs live at the apex of the power structure, and peons dwell at its bottom. In worldly endeavors, ranking serves its purpose, maintains order, and keeps freshmen and sophomores humble.

When it comes to spirituality, however, hierarchy distances people from their wholeness. You may have been taught the following:

- There are many levels between you and God.

- You dwell at the bottom stratum.

- If you can work your way up the ranks by doing good deeds, you can win the cosmic game of chutes and ladders.

- You can offset or bypass bad karma or get what you want by gaining the intercession of someone at a higher rank than you.

- You have one lifetime to get it right, otherwise you are consigned to a horrible hell forever.

If this sounds like a stacked deck or a bad deal, it *is*. Now for the good news: there's a new sheriff in town, and he doesn't pack a six-shooter.

Spirituality is more concentric than hierarchical. God does not sit at the top of a ladder you must climb. God dwells at the center of a circle, and you stand at its circumference. You also live at the center of the circle,

> God [is] a circle whose center [is] everywhere, and its circumference nowhere.
> — Ralph Waldo Emerson, quoting St. Augustine

where the deepest part of you is one with your source. If God is the sun, you are a ray. The ray is not all of the sun, but it contains all of its qualities. The sun embodies warmth, light, and energy; and so does the ray. Everything God is, you are. Everything God is not, you are not. Never speak about yourself in a way you would not speak about God. If you do, you are giving God a bad rap.

Everyone at the circumference of the circle of light has equal and direct connection to the source at its center. One dot at the edge of the circle will not get any closer to the center by going through another dot at the edge. If you want to connect with your source, you don't need to keep working your way around the periphery. Simply go within.

God is life, and everything that lives is an expression of God. Religions that believe they are closer to God than others have missed the point that the point is everywhere.

A man came to a guru and told him, "I will give you an orange if you can tell me where God is."

The guru replied, "I will give you two oranges if you can tell me where God is not."

You can make up a story that you are disconnected from the source of life, but if you are alive, you are connected. That source loves and supports you so much that you can even believe and live as if you are separate from it, and you will remain connected. The only place separation seems real is in the human mind.

Religions, schools, and society have taught you all kinds of cockamamie things about how bad you are, how angry God is, how much you need saving, and how scorched you will get in Hades. None of these are true. God is love, and you are eternally an expression

> If God is who our Sunday-school teachers told us He is, He could use a course in anger management.
> — Source unknown

of love and a receiver of it. Everything else is a bad dream from which you are awakening.

How Much Does Heaven Cost?

Perhaps you have heard about the Jewish rabbi who met a Catholic cardinal at a religious conference, and the two became friends. The cardinal invited the rabbi to visit the Vatican, where the rabbi noticed a golden telephone on an ornate altar.

"What do you use that telephone for?" the rabbi inquired.

"That's our direct hotline to God," the cardinal answered. "You can use it, but it's a long-distance call. It will cost you $100."

A few months later the cardinal was visiting the rabbi in Israel. In the synagogue office he noticed a plain telephone on a table in the corner. When the cardinal inquired about it, the rabbi explained, "We also have a direct line to God. Please use it if you like."

"How much does it cost?" asked the cardinal.

"Nothing," answered the rabbi. "It's a local call."

You have been taught that healing, enlightenment, success, and well-being are going to cost you. Some teachers, doctors, and organizations tell you that if you want to get well and be happy, you will have to go through a long, difficult, and expensive process. This directive plays on your belief that payment is required for healing. Other teachers and organizations tell you that happiness, health, and well-being are available to you right now if you choose. Enlightenment is free. Endarkenment costs.

A healer does not give a patient anything he or she does not already have. A healer simply awakens a part of the patient that has been sleeping. The power to heal is yours already. You can use external sources as "permission slips," but they are simply characters in the movie for which *you* have written the script. Whatever outside sources do *to* you or *for* you, you do to or for yourself.

A guru is someone who sits by the side of a river selling bottled river water. An inferior guru tells you, "I am your only connection to river water. Follow me, pay me, and I will keep you supplied with the source of life." A superior guru tells you, "If you like the water I have given you, I will show you the way to the river from which you can draw all you want for yourself." A true teacher or healer seeks to put him- or herself out of a job. Success is defined as the student's recognition of self-sufficiency.

The Power of Invocation

There do exist people, energies, and entities to whom you can appeal for support. I believe in the power of angels, spirit guides, *devas*, saints, and gurus; and I have experienced the blessing of help from above. We live in a vast, multidimensional universe—to restrict life to the very small bandwidth of humanity is egotism

> Miracles . . . are performed by those who temporarily have more for those who temporarily have less.
> — *A Course in Miracles*

taken to absurdity. People have been praying to demigods, guardians, and patron saints for thousands of years, and receiving healing and miracles.

If you are in fear, pain, or confusion, and you believe that a nonphysical source can help you, calling on that entity or energy is wise indeed. Just remember that such guides do not give you something you have not already got; they serve as a pipeline to your memory of it.

We have all attended public events where a minister speaks an invocation. While most people think of this as a sort of rote, obligatory prayer to be put up with while waiting for the meal or game to start, true invocation offers you immense spiritual power. Invocation means that you align your thoughts, feelings, and consciousness with a being or force that embodies characteristics you want or need.

If you desire to be more compassionate, you might call on the grace of Mother Mary. If you are a Hindu facing a challenge, you might invoke the presence of Ganesha, the overcomer of obstacles. In the Native American tradition, if you need wisdom and guidance, you might summon owl medicine. If you have a relationship with your guardian angel, you might ask him or her for protection.

On one level, you are asking external beings or entities for help. They are as real as anyone or anything you know—in some ways even more real than the three-dimensional forms the five senses show you. On another level, you are tapping into the power they represent. Angels, saints, demigods, and native medicine are aspects of your own divine nature. If you cannot accept your own enlightened identity, you may do better to relate to enlightenment or healing through others. No matter whether you go within yourself for healing or through an external channel, when you align with divinity, you have tapped into the font of your true strength.

Mister Rogers' Bigger Neighborhood

Keith Varnum worked as an intern on the set of the celebrated television show *Mister Rogers' Neighborhood*. Keith recounts that some of the stagehands made fun of Fred Rogers behind his back. The big, tough guys, Keith surmises, seemed threatened by Mr. Rogers's gentle ways.

Their mockery evaporated, however, when during rehearsal Mr. Rogers disappeared behind the puppet stage and worked a set of puppets. Something about the puppet theater felt safe to the stagehands, and they delved into sensitive personal discussions and asked the puppets for advice. Meanwhile Mr. Rogers was behind the scenes, delivering wisdom and compassion to these fellows through the venue of the puppet theater.

This odd scenario symbolizes how many of us relate to our Higher Power. We have been taught that God is a wrathful, punitive entity to be feared. Because God is invisible to the eye, or because we blame God for misfortunes, we may have difficulty relating to a Higher Power. Yet when someone appears in a body as a person we can relate to, we are more likely to trust and communicate with the divine through that form. In this sense, a Jesus, Moses, Buddha, Krishna, Mohammed, or any great prophet or guru may serve as a comfortable way for us to connect with God.

Can you have a personal relationship with God and communicate directly? Indeed you can, as easily as the stagehands could have had a relationship with Mr. Rogers if they were not threatened by him or they did not hold judgments about him. Each of us has our own relationship with our Higher Power. Take comfort in yours as you support and allow others to find guidance and healing in theirs.

Living the New Paradigm

We are entering a new era based upon a broader, deeper recognition of worthiness, entitlement, and empowerment. For a time it may seem that you need to appeal to others for help, and that is fine. But the time will come when you disconnect the human umbilicus and reattach the divine umbilicus. Then you will approach God from an attitude of *worthship,* not worship. When you are lost in the dream of separation, you pray *to* God; when unity is restored to your mind, you pray *from* God.

> Be humble before Him, and yet great *in* Him.
> — *A Course in Miracles*

We are told that Jesus said, "whoever believes in me, those works which I have done he will also do, and he will do greater works than these . . ." (John 14:12). To whom was Jesus referring? Not the limited, struggling, human self. He was addressing the greatness in you, your nature equal to his own. Jesus or any other savior is effective only if we are saved from the illusion of being small, weak, and separated from love. When we embrace our disowned selves and reclaim our wholeness, we look not *up* to others, but *in* to our true self.

As old beliefs and institutions fall away, you will find wisdom and power within you that you once believed you had to import. Then you will not need to fire the in-betweeners, because there will be no one or no thing between you and the fulfillment

> . . . be free, all worthy spirits,
> And stretch yourselves for greatness and for height.
> — George Chapman

you seek. You have been taught that you are a miserable sinner and you need someone closer to God to save you. But no one is closer to God than you at your true nature, and salvation comes not through a person, but from awakening. Your authentic self is as much a part of God as is any angel, *deva,* guru, saint, or spiritual entity. You are not subservient to such beings; you walk side by side with them. Then will come the great *infolding* as you reclaim all that you have projected as being outside yourself. At that moment you will simultaneously stand at the center of the universe and on the leading edge of its ongoing creation.

22

HIDING IN COMPLEXITY

Simplicity is the ultimate sophistication.

— ATTRIBUTED TO **LEONARDO DA VINCI**

I had a friend named Carey who had a way of complicating arguments so they would go on for a long time and nobody would win. He would drag in all kinds of irrelevant information and go off on tangents that left me scratching my head, wondering, *What were we talking about anyway?* Eventually I gave up trying to win arguments, and just prayed to resolve the issue at hand. Even that was difficult.

Carey had developed a propensity to hide in complexity when he grew up as a child of an alcoholic and needed to feel safe from being hurt. So he learned to weave tangled webs around himself to keep people at a distance and avoid being wounded. He succeeded at staying safe but lost at being present. His mind and life were so layered with complications that he rarely saw the light they were covering.

One day Carey and I participated in a seminar led by an intuitive healer named Mary. Mary led an exercise in which each class member was asked to stand in the center of the group and improvise a silent dance or mime. When it was Carey's turn, he stood in the circle by himself for a few moments and then began to pull people from the circle to join him. "Ah!" Mary commented. "Hiding in complexity!"

If Carey felt safe to be himself, he would not need to weave a camouflage to crouch behind. His value was not the problem—he was a great guy—but his *perception* of his value was shaky, so he had to don a costume to escape from being exposed. But the self he was hiding was not his true self. Only the false self seeks to hide. The best thing that could ever happen to Carey (like all of us) would be to recognize that his true self was lovable and valuable, and it did not need a thicket of complexity to disguise it.

Caves in the Mountains

Much of our society—especially government, law, medicine, economics, religion, and the corporate world—has piled layers upon layers of density to obscure what could easily be said or done in a simpler way. While some of these disciplines are complex by nature, practitioners often use their esoteric caves in their mountains to shield themselves from exposure.

The 2008 worldwide economic crisis offers a dramatic example of the ill effects of hiding in complexity. The crash occurred primarily because banks kept loaning more and more money to less-than-qualified borrowers, and leveraged themselves to a point where in some cases the institutions' debt-to-asset ratio was as high as 30 to 1. When the volume of defaulting borrowers reached a tipping point, the house of cards caved in. The downfall was set up when mortgage lenders loaned money to unstable households and then sold the notes to larger investment banks, who then consolidated the mortgages with car, student, and credit-card loans into bulk collateralized debt obligations (CDOs), which were then sold to investors all around the world.

No one in this chain of sale was at risk except the final holder, who by that time had completely lost track of the ill health of the original loan. Meanwhile each of the middlemen was making money on the transactions. As real estate values in America skyrocketed (doubling between 1996 and 2006), many financiers compromised integrity to close the sale. Lenders engaged in subprime high-interest loans, lending to risky borrowers at as little as .07 percent down and 99.3 percent financing. If the borrower succumbed to foreclosure, he could walk away with virtually no loss, leaving the bank with an unsellable property in a depressed market. Banks paid billions of dollars to Wall Street rating agencies, which gave them solid reviews even as they were collapsing. Banks were simultaneously selling loans and taking out huge insurance policies, betting that their borrowers would default, then collecting on claims when that occurred. This system offered so many illicit angles to turn a profit and so many places to hide that it became a runaway horse no one could harness.

Robert Gnaizda, director of consumer-advocacy agency Greenlining Institute, called Secretary of the Treasury Alan Greenspan's attention to 150 complex adjustable mortgages by one lender alone. Gnaizda reports that Greenspan commented, "If you had a doctorate in math, you wouldn't be able to understand which was good for you and which wasn't."

Yet the balance of nature will not perpetuate a system that defies integrity. Because the financial system was not sound, it had to crash. None of us enjoyed participating in the process, but ultimately it was a course correction toward fewer hiding places and more responsible investing.

The universe is not against complexity. Creation is complex beyond human understanding. The universe will just not put up with hiding in complexity, using a functional system for dysfunctional purposes. The nature of bubbles is to burst. The nature of healthy seeds planted in fertile ground is to grow. At every moment we are choosing whether to ride on a bubble or send our roots into solid ground.

How Simple Can It Get?

When Henry David Thoreau returned from his famous sojourn at Walden Pond, he paid a visit to Ralph Waldo Emerson (who owned the Walden property and had rented it to Thoreau). "What did you learn from your retreat?" Emerson asked Thoreau.

"Simplify, simplify, simplify," Thoreau answered proudly.

"Hmm," Emerson replied. "One 'simplify' would have been quite sufficient."

The closer a statement is to the truth, the more simply it is expressed. The more words, the more moving parts, the more rules, the more sleight of hand, the more experts required to interpret . . . the more room for hiding and manipulation.

> The truth is simple. If it were complicated, everyone would understand it.
> — Source unknown

You can assess the integrity of a statement, person, or system by how many layers you need to plumb to get to the truth behind it. Perhaps you have had the experience of being with someone you love, and your communication is complete without words. If you

> He who says does not know.
> He who knows does not say.
> — Lao-tzu

try to use words, you diminish the pristine quality of the moment. Words can express the truth, but more often they are a substitute or distraction from it.

Real communication is energetic and has little to do with verbiage. If you want to do a rewarding experiment, see how few words you really need in order to say what you need to say. You will be amazed by how strong and clear your communication becomes when you say more by saying less. You will also be astounded by all the extraneous, meaningless, distracting words passing between people.

A web-design expert told me, "After you design your home page, go back and eliminate 50 percent of the words. Then go back and eliminate another 50 percent of the words. Then you will have an effective home page."

I have learned the same principle when editors have asked me to cut back the number of words in a book or article. I love to edit this way because I must get to the essence of what I want to say. I am always surprised by how many words I can remove and still get my point across.

As you practice making your words count, you may find yourself becoming more telepathic. In *Mutant Message Down Under,* Marlo Morgan describes her walkabout with an Aboriginal tribe in Australia. During that sojourn the tribespeople spoke little and sang a lot. Most of their communication was psychic. They told Marlo that the purpose of the voice is singing, and real communication is from mind to mind, heart to heart.

Where to Search

Nasrudin's neighbor came home one evening to find Nasrudin on his hands and knees under a streetlight, searching for some object. "Did you lose something?" the fellow asked.

"My house key," Nasrudin explained.

Wanting to be of service, the neighbor got down on the ground with Nasrudin and helped him pick through the grass. Half an hour later the neighbor asked, "Do you remember where you dropped it?"

"Over there," answered Nasrudin, pointing to a spot many yards away, near his doorstep.

Stunned, the neighbor stood up and asked, "Then why are you looking here?"

"Because there is more light here," Nasrudin answered.

Sometimes there seems to be more light where everyone is looking, even if no one is finding.

> If you take enough people to the middle of nowhere, it starts to feel like somewhere.
> — Auto advertisement

According to *A Course in Miracles,* the ego created the world as a hiding place, and the values of the world are the direct opposite of truth. The *Course* further states that if you want to know the truth, reverse everything the world has taught you.

> It's the best possible time to be alive, when almost everything you thought you knew is wrong.
> — Tom Stoppard

If you have not found solace in complexity, try simplicity. You might just find your lost key right where you left it.

As the world becomes more and more complicated, simplicity shines more brightly by contrast. Those who have an investment in hiding in complexity weave convoluted games and systems to conceal their spoils, while those who find clarity more attractive will exit the caves of illusion and find their way to the sun. Runaway complexity wins only a losing game, for no one escapes the web woven to entrap others. Those who trust the truth do not need to cover it up. They stand confidently upon it.

23

THE BEST
DEFENSE

Your defenses will not work, but you are not in danger.

— *A COURSE IN MIRACLES*

During a war in Beirut, Lebanon, Mother Teresa announced that she was going to enter the combat zone to rescue children from a hospital in the center of the city. When the warring factions learned of the nun's intentions, they declared a cease-fire. I saw a video of Mother Teresa and her assistants proceeding in a truck through the streets, soldiers standing quietly aside. The nuns entered the hospital, removed the children, and drove out of Beirut. As soon as the truck passed the city limits, the armies began shooting at each other again.

Behold the power of one person's faith and love to disarm a war. One person connected to a Higher Power is stronger than many who are disconnected. Manifestation of well-being is not a matter of mass or prowess; it is a matter of

> The pure, unadulterated love of one person can nullify the hatred of millions.
> — attributed to Mahatma Gandhi

intention and alignment with universal truth. Safety is not created by armaments. It is created by love.

We all spend a significant amount of time, energy, and money defending and protecting ourselves. We lock our homes and cars, insure our bodies and possessions, and erect fences around our borders. We wear seat belts, apply fabric protectors to our sofas, douse our skin with high-SPF sunscreen, and use condoms to prevent unwanted pregnancies. We inoculate our bodies against viruses and buffer our computers with firewalls. We call the police if we suspect a prowler in the neighborhood, obtain restraining orders against intrusive exes, and pay taxes on our airline tickets toward airport security. In 2010, the U.S. Government spent $847 billion, or about 25 percent of tax dollars, on defense.

On a more personal level, we argue when insulted and go to great efforts to convince others that we are right. We are drawn to religions that promise to save us from the ravages of hell if we follow prescribed dogma. We lecture our teenagers to avoid the wrong crowd, and we deploy them with GPS-embedded cell phones so we can track their whereabouts. We attend football games and shout at the top of our lungs, "DE-FENSE! DE-FENSE! DE-FENSE!"

While some of these precautions are useful and warranted, a liberating question to ask yourself might be: *"How much defense and protection do I really need?"*

Does life really require so many precautions? What makes a person safe?

After my friend Bette was diagnosed with cancer, she decided to make her life a journey of trust. She would leave her car in New Jersey mall parking lots with the doors unlocked and the key in the ignition. One day she picked up a hitchhiker who told her he was going home to reconcile with his wife after they had argued and he had run off. Bette was so moved by the fellow's intention that she offered him her new car to make the trip. The man dropped Bette off at her home and promised to return her car that evening. When he did not show up at the appointed time, Bette wondered if she had made a big mistake. A few hours later the fellow arrived with his wife, who tearfully thanked Bette for her generosity in helping them reconnect.

I'm not suggesting that you leave your car with the keys in it or loan it to strangers, unless you feel so guided. I *am* suggesting that you have a source of protection that goes far beyond car keys. When you recognize, as *A Course in Miracles* reminds us, "In my defenselessness my safety lies," the notion of self-protection gives way to deep internal security—the "peace . . . which passes understanding" (Philippians 4:7).

Trimming the Bylaws

When my friend Lora accepted the position as minister of a church, her first act was to ask the board of trustees to review the church's bylaws and remove any elements based on fear or protectionism. The board rose to the task, and when they were finished, they had whittled a 43-page document down to 18 pages.

While contracts serve their purpose, they are more often monuments to fear than a vision of a positive outcome. The first time I took out a mortgage on a home many years ago, the paperwork involved perhaps 25 pages. When I recently refinanced, I found more than 70 pages to review, initial, and sign. At some point the weight of mortgage documents will exceed that of the house! Every time a lender gets burned by someone, they add another page to protect themselves from a repeat of the incident.

I went through a similar process when I began to present seminars. Originally I simply made a verbal deal with a sponsor, and I showed up on a handshake. Over time as sponsors either misunderstood our deal or did not honor it, I added protective clauses to the contract. One day when I noticed how cumbersome and fear laden the document had become, I decided that it did not represent the kind of energy I wanted to underpin my transactions. So I pared the contract down to the simplest and most basic terms, and decided to trust when it came to the others. That highly streamlined contract has served well for many years, and I do not miss the extra papers or protective clauses. Now I often rely simply on verbal agreements or a short e-mail summary.

Fear and Trust

Do your chosen defenses cost you more than they net you? I know a fellow who, when he parks his car on a city street, writes down the license-plate numbers of the cars in front of him and behind him, in case one of them bumps his car while exiting. While this practice makes him feel safe, one must wonder if the time and effort are really worth it, and if his mind-set of fear is adding to the quality of life or detracting from it.

Fear and self-protection have become dominant themes in many industries. Many doctors in certain states are either leaving medicine or the state because the malpractice-insurance premiums are so high that these physicians cannot make a decent living. An M.D. friend of mine decided he had had enough of a fear-based system, and he announced to his friends and patients that he was no longer going to carry malpractice insurance. "I am going to trust that I can serve my patients without anyone suing me," he declared. While some may consider such a doctor a dreamer, his faith has sustained him thus far. Perhaps he is contributing to a new vision that may ultimately transform a system in which panic has encroached on healing.

I am not suggesting that you drop all forms of defense, especially if they give you a feeling of safety. You have to be at peace with your beliefs and values. I *am* suggesting that you examine which defenses you really need, and consider gradually reducing your sense of need for protection. A good piece of introspection would be: "What do I really need to protect? Why? Where and what is the source of real protection?"

Defenses Attract What They Defend Against

When your consciousness is steeped in defense, you are fixated on undesirable outcomes. The more you focus on undesirable outcomes, the more you tend to attract what you resist. Defenses do not make the things you resist go away; they magnify them in your experience.

A recently married couple named Tim and Lona attended one of my residential seminars. In their 40s, they had both been married previously. During the seminar Lona became extremely jealous of Tim's interactions with other women in the group. From the observers' perspective, Tim's exchanges were innocent and in no way violated his marriage. Lona admitted that jealousy had been a big issue in her previous relationships, to the point of ruining them.

Lona's upset grew so intense that it spilled into our group process, and other participants tried to soothe her. One woman asked Lona a penetrating question: "Wouldn't it be a shame if you finally met a trustworthy man, but lost him because you didn't trust him?"

Within the year Tim and Lona divorced, and a few years later he remarried and started a family. Lona's fear of losing Tim and her attempts to defend her marriage ultimately pushed her husband away. Her defenses did what she defended against.

Often what is presented as defense is simply a cloaked offense. Adolf Hitler ignited World War II when he convinced the German people that if their country did not attack Poland first, Poland would attack them. The German war machine took aim at the world under the guise of being a preemptive strike, and caused tragic suffering for millions and the German nation itself.

When you hear "preemptive strike," remove "preemptive" from the phrase, and you will see that defenses against war *create* war.

Royal Disclosure

Those who drop defenses and pretenses offer a refreshing, healing, and liberating model for all who look upon them. I saw a candid interview with Princess Diana after she divorced Prince Charles. In the interview, she was extraordinarily honest about many issues she had concealed in her royal marriage, including her deteriorating relationship, her eating disorder, her extramarital love affair, and her husband's relationship with his own lover. I watched in awe, with deep respect for this woman who formerly had so much to lose by telling the truth, and now had so much to gain. When someone stands uncloaked in a world dominated by lying, hiding, and faux presentation, the light he or she shines exerts an extraordinary healing effect.

"The Emperor's New Clothes" is far more than a children's parable. It disrobes a world where illusions cloak the truth and mass hypnosis dulls our awareness of reality. The more we have invested in presentation, the weightier the armaments required to maintain the image. The more we trust truth, the less we need to appropriate to our personal defense budget. The world needs truth more than protection. Ultimate truth *is* protection, for it dissolves fear and lies by its presence.

> If you believe the doctors, nothing is wholesome; if you believe the theologians, nothing is innocent; if you believe the soldiers, nothing is safe.
> — Lord Salisbury

How to End Terrorism

At a U.S. Cavalry fort in the old West, soldiers had been holed up shooting at Indians for a long time until but two cavalrymen remained. Finally one soldier turned to the other and announced, "I have good news, and I have bad news."

"Let's have the bad news first," replied his buddy.

"The bad news is that we are out of ammunition, and there are no reinforcements."

"And the good news?"

"The good news is that there are no Indians."

When you create an enemy in your mind, everything you do to destroy it will destroy you. Wars against terror are wars *of* terror. The way to end terror, personally and globally, is to not be terri-fied. The place to end terrorism is within yourself. Inside your

> When planning revenge, dig two graves.
> — Chinese proverb

mind lives a terrorist in some ways more insidious than those you read about in the news. Every time you tell yourself a frightening thought and act on it, you are contributing to terrorism in the world. Every time you supplant a frightening thought with a sense of trust and inner peace, you defuse terrorism in the world.

If each of us refused to be afraid in our personal lives, there would be nothing for global terrorism to feed on. Don't wait for the government to end terrorism. Do it yourself, from the inside out. When you remove defensiveness from your consciousness, you bring the world closer to peace.

In 1949 Costa Rica was the first country in the world to abol-ish its standing army. Since that time 20 other countries have dis-banded their military forces. Such a concept seems foreign and threatening to the mind absorbed in defensiveness. Yet Costa Rica is thriv-ing, and has be-

> I think that people want peace so much that one of these days governments had better get out of the way and let them have it.
> — Dwight D. Eisenhower

come a center for world peace, the home of the Inter-American Court of Human Rights and the United Nations–mandated Uni-versity for Peace. Can you conceive of larger nations abolishing or significantly diminishing their armies and armaments? While such a vision may seem fantastic, consider that oppressive human institutions such as slavery and apartheid were once considered normal and acceptable, but the evolution of awakening has dis-solved them.

While you may not have the power to dissolve a nation's standing army, you do have the power to dissolve your own.

Consider how much more powerfully your energy can be spent in creative projects rather than defensive ones. Think less about what you might lose by letting go of fear, and what you might gain by practicing trust. Defenselessness is not an attribute of the weak. It is the hallmark of the courageous.

> Non-violence is the summit of bravery.
> — Mahatma Gandhi

24

WHAT YOU REALLY NEED

*You were given everything when you were created,
just as everyone was.*

— A COURSE IN MIRACLES

While visiting Omaha, Nebraska, my host Dave Wingert drove me past mega-billionaire Warren Buffett's house. To my surprise, the abode of "the Oracle of Omaha" looks pretty much like everyone else's home in the 'hood. Modest size, about three bedrooms. Tasteful landscaping. No porte cochere. No burgeoning fountains to rival Versailles. No fence, wall, driveway gate, security guard, or barking Dobermans. Several large bushes dot the perimeter of the property, not even a hedge, allowing passersby to see onto the grounds. Warren Buffett's home is anything but ostentatious or protected. It is as normal as normal gets.

Dave told me that Warren Buffett is a regular guy, known and loved in his hometown. He shows up at community plays, licks ice-cream cones at local sweetshops, and schmoozes amiably with local denizens. He still lives in the same house he bought after he got married over 50 years ago. "Everything I need is in that house," Warren says.

When Mr. Buffett gets home from work, he plops himself in front of the TV and snacks on popcorn. He tools around town in a car several years old, and he would not have a chauffeur or body-guard. He travels by private jet only rarely, despite the fact that he owns the world's largest private-jet company. He writes one letter each year to the CEOs of Berkshire Hathaway's 63 companies, de-lineating their annual goals. He holds no company meetings, and his CEOs rarely receive phone calls from him. Warren Buffett does not tote a cell phone, and his desk is devoid of a computer.

So lives the philanthropist who donated $37 billion to the Bill & Melinda Gates [charitable] Foundation and called a meeting of 20 of the world's richest men and convinced them to give half of their wealth to charity—*before* they die.

Warren Buffett's day-to-day life definitely does not match the over-the-top digs I have seen on *Lifestyles of the Rich and Famous*. It seems more like *Lifestyles of the Simply Grateful*. Is it possible that the purpose of life is not to accumulate money and stuff and prove that the guy who dies with the most toys wins? Would it feel bet-ter to just have what you love and love what you have?

Warren Buffett is one of my role models, as a man at peace with himself, his vocation, and his life. He owns his money; it does not own him. He uses what he needs and passes the rest along to help others. He offers a living model of "Right Livelihood."

The More You Know, the Less You Need

"Well, that's all fine and good for Warren Buffett," you say. "I wish I had billions of dollars to give away. Right now I'd be happy to be able to just pay my rent and keep up with the price of gas." *Got it.* If you would like to have a bank account more like Warren Buffett's, let's look at how he and other wealthy people grew theirs.

When Ted Turner donated a billion dollars to the United Nations, he declared, "The world is awash with money." Easy for him to say, right? He, too, has more money than he can count. Yet consider the mind-set Ted Turner had to have to attract that kind of wealth. Which came first: having billions of dollars, or believing that billions of dollars were waiting to be had? The latter, for sure.

Belief precedes manifestation. Yes, you believe what you get, but more fundamentally you get what you believe. What do you believe about money?

You may think you need money, and that may be true on the surface level of your life. Even more important, you need to know that the universe is capable of providing for all your needs, and the more you trust its support, the more good stuff shows up.

My friend Millie is a successful motivational teacher. One day she told me, "I have to get going now to teach my new class."

"Good luck," I told her.

"Thanks," Millie replied, "but I don't need luck. I'm programmed to succeed."

You and I, too, don't need luck as much as we need a *success mentality.* The more you recognize that prosperity is your natural state, the less you need to struggle to import your good. If you think you are empty and broken, you will be a bottomless pool of need, and nothing in the outer world will be able to fill the *perceived* pit within you. If you know you are loved and supported by the universe, nothing in the outer world can add to or take away from your wealth. You are either whole or you are not. You are either secure or you are not. There is either enough or there is not. There is an inverse relationship between wisdom and need. When you know how much you have, you know how little you need.

The De-manifestation Workshop

Many of us have spent a great deal of time, effort, and money learning to manifest things. We read books, go to seminars, pray, repeat affirmations, create treasure maps, and practice claiming the objects we want and deserve. These methods really work! We obtain our mate, house, and car . . . and the latest-generation iPod, iPhone, iPad, and lots of other groovy i-paraphernalia.

Yet there is a pattern I notice among people who have accumulated lots of stuff (myself included). After a while you wish you had less stuff. You get tired of all the time, money, and angst it takes to manage stuff. You cease to be a stuff enjoyer, and you become a stuff manager.

Having stuff is not as simple as it appears. You have to get the money to buy it; keep it clean and repaired; protect and insure it; make sure other people don't misuse, break, or steal it; move it when you move; store it; and then figure out what to do with it when you are done with it. When your original stuff becomes obsolete (sometimes shortly after you purchase it), you have to get the next latest and greatest

> What you possess, possesses you.
> — Jidda Krishnamurti

version. If you went into debt to purchase your stuff, you have to go to work to keep up with the payments, and if you don't like your job, you feel burdened or enslaved. You fight over stuff with people you used to get along with, and you envy people who have stuff you want but can't get. You have to figure out who will get your stuff when you die, and then your heirs turn your legacy into a tug-of-war. Eventually the manifestation workshop doesn't seem so attractive to you anymore. You are ready for the *de*-manifestation workshop!

Consider the yogi who asked his guru, "How can I become enlightened?"

"Find a cave, sit naked, and meditate," the guru advised him.

Eager for illumination, the yogi found a cave and followed the guru's instructions—except for the naked part. That was a little too much to ask. So he took along a loincloth.

The yogi sat in deep meditation for several days, and what bliss he felt! The guru's advice was obviously divinely inspired.

When he arose, the yogi needed to wash his loincloth. So he rinsed it in the local stream and hung it out to dry. When he went to retrieve it, he noticed that some mice had chewed holes in it.

So the yogi went into town, where he procured a cat to get rid of the mice.

That worked for a while, but for the cat to stay around, it needed milk. So the yogi went back into town and found a cow. But he had to stay there for a few weeks to earn the money to purchase it. He missed his meditation practice, but told himself that this was just a temporary distraction and ultimately having the cow and cat would help keep his loincloth intact.

The yogi brought the cow back and fed the cat, which kept the mice away and afforded him some more time for meditation.

But the cow needed to be fed and milked, and this was all too much for the yogi to take care of by himself. So he decided to get a wife. (Pre–women's movement, you understand.) The wife, however, was not content to live in a cave, so the yogi took a job and earned the money to build a house. Then children came, and you know what comes along with that.

Long story short (I know it's too late for that), eventually the yogi had a family, house, farm, and business, and he could find hardly a moment to meditate and cultivate inner peace.

One day the (former) yogi heard a knock on his door. There, to his astonishment, stood the guru who had dispatched him on his meditation mission. The yogi looked so different that the guru did not recognize him. "Excuse me," he said, "can you tell me where I can find the yogi who used to meditate in that cave over there?"

"That's me!" the householder explained.

"What happened to your quest for enlightenment?" the guru asked.

"I took a loincloth!"

⌒

Stuff is fun, and stuff is cool. The question is: *Do you own your stuff, or does your stuff own you?* Here is the golden rule for how much stuff to have:

Have as much stuff as you can enjoy and manage peacefully.

Review your possessions and ask yourself, "Does owning this item bring me more joy, or angst? Do I feel freer for having this, or more bound?"

If your item brings you joy and freedom, keep it. If it brings you more angst or bondage, get rid of it. You cannot afford anything that distracts you from peace. Each of us must find our

> What gift could I prefer before the peace of God?
> — A Course in Miracles

own niche in life. Some people do well with a little stuff, and others do well with a lot of stuff. In the end, stuff doesn't matter. Only happiness matters. If you can manifest stuff, you are doing well. If you can manifest peace, you are doing better.

Enough Is Enough

When I visited Israel after graduating college, I stumbled upon a delightful little café tucked in a basement in a backstreet in Tel Aviv. The modest shop was overflowing with night birds savoring homemade coffee and exotic tea, delectable pastries, and ambient live music. A line outside the door attested to the popularity of the place.

As I was leaving, I met the owner, a 30-ish woman who had established the eatery with her husband. She was busy but smiling. "This is a great place you have here," I told her. "You should expand and open up some more shops around town."

The woman smiled and shook her head. "No thanks," she replied. "This isn't New York."

I was stunned by her response. Why wouldn't she cash in on a great opportunity? Yet as I have pondered her statement over many years, I have grown to understand and respect it. Her shop was successful; she was enjoying it; she knew her patrons; and the responsibility of the business was as much as she wanted to handle, or could. In her world, satisfaction was more important than expansion.

Expansion can certainly be satisfying and worthwhile. Our nature is to grow beyond old limits and master uncharted territory. The question is: *Does expanding your business increase the quality of your life, or diminish it?*

Sometimes more money means more happiness, and sometimes it doesn't. Some small mom-and-pop businesses have grown to corporate and national levels and retained their intention of joy and service. Many don't. Going public doesn't always mean going peaceful. If you are considering expansion, be sure that you do it in a way that maintains the quality of life you now savor.

The Illusion of Need

Let's fast-forward to the ultimate lesson about need: *You don't have any.* Not really. Sure, on a physical level you need food, water, and shelter. You can also cite emotional and financial needs that come with living in the world. Yet on the deepest level of your spiritual being, you already contain, and are, everything you need. You don't need anything from the outside world, because you already own and are it on the inside world.

This may sound outlandish, but remember that *claiming contentment is a radical act.* You will not find the truth of *enough* advertised on television, in glamour magazines, or at the board meeting. Nearly all of those media are based on something being wrong with you or the world, or the drive for more, more, more. Very few people drive themselves for enough, enough, enough. The world as you have been taught to know it is based on the belief in lack. Shift your vision to supply and you will see a very different world.

If you have needs in the world, they will be met. My favorite Bible passage is Psalm 23. At its conclusion we are reminded, "Surely goodness and mercy shall follow me all the days of my life." When I meditate on that passage, I realize that goodness and mercy *have* followed me all the days of my life. I have been spiritually asleep for a great portion of my journey, and done lots of foolish things. Yet in spite of my human ineptitude, a divine spark within me keeps waking me when I doze, impeccable intelligence keeps guiding me back onto my path when I detour, and a love that transcends pain keeps forgiving me when I err.

As I look back on my journey, I recognize that every need I have ever had has been filled, either by having my desired object show up or something better coming along, or by realizing that I didn't really need what I thought I did. I have usually received *more* than I asked for because the universe had a bigger idea for me than I had for myself. In that sense, need is an illusion and fulfillment a reality.

Warren Buffett is a wealthy man not because he has billions of dollars, but because he has kept his spirit alive. He has enough because he *started* with the idea that there is enough. The richest man in the world is an exception to the economy of lack, and the ultimate demonstration of the economy of supply. Both economies exist simultaneously, each populated by those who subscribe to it. Each is available now. Your only true need is to remember that your needs are truly met.

25

THE SECRET TO WINNING THE LOTTERY

Infinite riches in a little room.

— CHRISTOPHER MARLOWE

Just before Christmas, Rob Anderson went into a convenience store to purchase three $1 Powerball lottery tickets as stocking stuffers. The clerk misunderstood Anderson's request and erroneously printed one $3 ticket. When Rob called the mistake to the clerk's attention, the clerk offered to nullify the ticket. Rob decided to just go with what was happening, so he accepted the ticket and purchased the three stocking stuffers in addition. Anderson went home and tossed the "mistake" ticket on his nightstand.

The day after Christmas the winning numbers were announced, and Rob figured he would check the mistake ticket just in case. It was then that he realized the mistake was no mistake. He had just won nearly $129 million, the largest Powerball jackpot ever paid in the Kentucky lottery.

There's a secret to good fortune, which, like many of the world's best-kept secrets, remains hidden because it is so obvious. The secret to winning the lottery is simple: you've already won.

Now you might be tempted to argue that your bank account doesn't quite reflect such wealth. Understood. Yet, like Nasrudin crawling beneath the lamppost searching for his key far from where he dropped it, you might be looking in the wrong place for your winnings. Look a little deeper and you might discover a cache of riches with your name already on it.

Psychologists have done numerous studies of lottery winners, with fascinating findings. Many lottery winners experience severely negative psychological results, including depression, alcoholism, and suicide. (Some states have support groups for lottery winners.) A friend of mine won $6 million in a state lottery, and she subsequently spent a great deal of time and energy fending off her ex-husband's claim on the money, turning down loan requests from friends she hadn't seen in many years, and hiring a bodyguard to safeguard her son from kidnapping. So winning the lottery is not necessarily a trip to heaven. It can mean a trip to hell.

Yet the study I find most interesting is this: Lottery winners who were happy *before* they won were happy *after* winning. Lottery winners who were *un*happy before they won grew more unhappy afterward. So the secret to winning the lottery is to find abundance and well-being right where you stand. If you need the lottery money to make you happy, you've lost before you've begun. If winning the lottery is the next fun step on your expanding adventure of abundance, you win big-time.

Winning the lottery does not cause happiness. Only the choice to be happy causes happiness.

The Gold You Own

My coaching client Ben, a successful architect, has a son and daughter who are struggling in careers in art and acting. Ben was frustrated because his kids were not making ends meet or taking his advice to choose professional career tracks he believed would net them greater success and income.

"My kids are smart, healthy, and kind," Ben told me. "We have always had a great relationship. They are honest, creative, and want to make a contribution to the world. When I told my son and daughter that I am planning to retire and may not be able to keep giving them stipends, they both volunteered to work harder, even get second jobs, to balance their accounts. My son is just a happy guy; nothing can get him down. My daughter is also very well adjusted."

I stopped Ben right there. "Do you realize how successful you and your children are?" I asked him. "You have raised two fine young adults who are exploring highly creative careers and growing as they go. They are mature, respectful, and close with your family. You love them and they love you. They are among the best-functioning segment of the population. You, sir, already own the gold you seek."

Tears welled up in Ben's eyes. "I know you're right," he told me. "I've been overlooking the riches I already own. I couldn't ask for better children. It's not their happiness I need to address. It's my own."

Mistakes in Your Favor

When Rob Anderson told the convenience-store cashier he didn't need to void the ticket he had printed "by mistake," Rob became $129 million richer. He decided to accept the event as possibly serving his good. Could things that seem to be going wrong really be going right? Might the universe be conspiring in your favor?

The word *conspiracy* comes from the Latin *conspirare*, meaning "to breathe together." Often we associate "conspiracy" with an underground movement to overthrow an established order. But the word has a far deeper meaning that can empower you as you understand it. When you breathe together with the universe, you find that it is working on your behalf. You don't have to subvert the established order, because universal order is already set up for you to succeed.

Our pain derives not from what happens, but from resisting what happens and not letting life be as it is. When we can accept the current of events (a form of *currency*) and look for ways that change serves us, what we thought was a curse becomes a blessing . . . a hardship becomes a starship.

A few years ago I needed to move my office. I found a new site that was not ideal, with small rooms, far from my home, and near a noisy intersection. But I had a time crunch for moving and the place seemed adequate, so I told the Realtor I would take it.

Weeks passed and I did not hear from the Realtor. Since I needed to vacate my old office, I phoned the agent to ask him if he had a lease for me to sign. He sheepishly told me that the landlord did not want to rent to me because he had read one of my books and he did not agree with my philosophy.

I felt outraged. "That's discrimination!" I complained. The Realtor agreed, but suggested that it would probably not be worth my while to fight it.

On my way home from work that day, I felt an inclination to take a scenic route on a lesser-traveled country road. Along the way I noticed a storefront with a FOR RENT sign in the window. I inquired with the landlady, who was quite congenial and informed me that the space had last been used as a tai chi studio. The rent was far less than the office I had planned to lease, and the space was larger, close to my home, and in a quiet area. I rented the site on the spot, and enjoyed years of good use of that facility.

What I thought was my winning lottery ticket (the space from which I was rejected) was actually not the winner I sought. The "loss" of that space directed me to the real winning

> Rejection is protection.
> — Source unknown

ticket. The timing was perfect, because the place in the country had not been vacant when I told the Realtor I would rent the less desirable space. The universe was conspiring in my favor, and when I was willing to breathe with it, I found all that I needed and more.

What's Fair Is Fair

People who have an abundance mentality keep attracting more of what they want and need. Those with a lack mentality keep attracting something missing. People who celebrate what they have already won, win more. Those who complain about what they have lost, keep losing. The law of consciousness is consistent.

My friend Hannah thrives in her business and is quite wealthy. She likes to earn money, enjoys making win-win deals, treats herself well, and is very generous. Hannah learned that Oprah Winfrey was offering a seminar for a small group of deserving women, most of whom would be selected on the basis of an essay they submitted on "Why I Need a Spa Retreat with Oprah." Another handful would be chosen by a lottery. Hannah very much wanted a trip with Oprah, but knew she could not with integrity say she needed one, so she submitted her name to the lottery. A month later she received a phone call from Oprah's office informing her that she had won. Hannah attended the seminar, received immense benefit from it, and the program was later aired on *The Oprah Winfrey Show.*

You might say that it wasn't fair for a wealthy woman to win the Oprah lottery. But consider *why* Hannah is prosperous and successful. She has an abundance consciousness. She thinks and lives success, so more success finds her. It will find you, too, if you claim it where you stand.

Don't Wait for Oprah

If you want to be rich and famous and help a lot of people, don't sit around and wait for Oprah to discover you. A friend told me, "I just know that when Oprah finds my book and holds it up on her television show, all of my dreams will come true."

It occurred to me that Oprah Winfrey has become the new lottery, the knight in shining armor who will sweep you away from diapers and car payments and make everything all right. If you watch Oprah's show, however, you will discover that she chooses guests who have found wealth, wholeness, and opportunities to serve right where they are. If you expect to win the Oprah lottery, you will need to first make the most of your life as it is.

Don't wait to win any lottery to become happy. Win it by *being* happy. Align your thoughts, feelings, words, and acts with a success attitude, and positive events will follow. Losers don't win the lottery. If they do, they quickly revert to loser status. Winners can never become losers, because they win wherever they are. Your life will succeed not because a windfall drops in your lap. Your life will succeed because you drop into your heart. Then windfalls will find you without your having to depend on them.

Your winning ticket has been printed. It is not a mistake. Will you keep it?

26

TIME
ENOUGH

But what minutes! Count them by sensation,
and not by calendars, and each moment is a day . . .

— BENJAMIN DISRAELI

Do you wish you had more time? Do you rush to get places, leave projects until the last minute, miss deadlines, apologize for being late, and watch the clock more than feel your spirit? Do you become stressed or frazzled because there is just not enough time to get everything done?

If so, I have good news for you. You can find more time by transforming your *relationship* with time. The answer to time stress is not logistical. It is attitudinal. You actually have enough time to do everything you need to do. Let's look at why this is so and how you can transform time to become your valued friend.

An Abundance of Time

I have said that every thought and feeling you experience proceeds from either a belief in supply or a belief in lack. Time is no exception. The amount of time you perceive is as small or expansive as your thoughts about it. I discovered this principle when I was constantly running late; I believed there were just not enough minutes in a day to do everything I needed to get done. If there were only another hour to negotiate traffic, another day to complete the project, or another week of vacation, *then* I would have enough time.

Then I realized I was seeing time through a lens of lack. The universe, I believed, was abundant in all things except for time. There was just not enough of that. Suddenly I understood that time is not a management issue. It is an *abundance* issue. You can take courses in how to prioritize your time, buy organizer notebooks and software, and arrange your schedule to get your to-do list done—all of which help somewhat. But unless you shift your awareness from *lack* of time to *supply* of time, you will not get very far. You will just be rearranging chairs on the deck of a sinking ship. Plug the holes in your belief system out of which precious time is leaking. Mind-set is more important than manipulation; context supersedes content.

You are not a victim of lack of time; you are a victim of a time-poverty mentality. The good news about being the victim of a mentality is that you are also the victimizer, so you can choose to quit hurting yourself. The answer to time woes is in your head, a domain over which you have total control.

Elastic Time

Time as we experience it is an invention of the human mind. No creature in nature tells time the way we do. The sun and moon, plants and animals, and everything that lives and moves contain an impeccable internal knowing of what to do and when. Animals do not stress about waking up to get to work, and the moon does not check its watch to be sure it stays on its 29-day cycle. All of creation is in tune with natural rhythms, and everything gets done in perfect timing without fear, stress, resistance, deadlines, late notices, or penalties.

When Albert Einstein was asked to explain his theory of relativity so a layperson could understand it, he answered, "Sit with a pretty girl for an hour, and it seems like a minute. . . . *That's* relativity." A more graphic philosopher noted, "The length of a minute depends on which side of the bathroom door you find yourself."

When you are anxious, fearful, and impatient, time goes excruciatingly slowly and a minute feels like an hour. When you are enjoying yourself, hours zip by without your even noticing. In spite of the clocks that seem to define life, the *experience* of time depends on the consciousness from which you observe it.

Time is not solid, but elastic; it expands or contracts with your consciousness. Have you ever noticed that when you are in a rush to get somewhere, that's when you get behind slow drivers, hit all the red lights, and are halted by road-construction projects? By contrast, when you are relaxed and feeling in the flow, traffic is light, you cruise through a string of green lights, and you arrive early. It is said that "lovers make a fool of time," because when you are in love, you live in a consciousness that transcends time. In that buoyant state of mind, you are not bound by limiting thoughts and the world their projections engender. Being a lover does not mean simply to be in a romantic relationship. When you become a lover of life, time loses the power it once seemed to have over your world.

> Time is a dressmaker specializing in alterations.
> — Faith Baldwin

I once had to mail a package from Hawaii to my assistant in New Jersey. I arrived at the post office at 11:50 A.M. on a Saturday, ten minutes before closing, and handed my package to the clerk. "This box is not taped properly," he informed me. "You are going to have to tape it better before we can send it."

At that time the post office did not sell tape, so my only option was to drive to a store to purchase some. The closest store was in a shopping center a few blocks away, and there was no way

I would have enough time to get there and back before the post office closed. I was not about to rush like a madman to try. So I decided to make a game of it. I would relax and let the universe handle the details. I would set out to buy the tape, and if I got back to the post office on time, I would mail the package. If not, I would just wait until Monday. Stress was not an option.

I calmly drove through traffic to the store, making sure not to hurry or worry as I went. With a peaceful gait I walked into the store and learned that the office supplies were in the back. Okay, no rushing. I found the tape and proceeded to the checkout counter. (Along the way I grabbed some laundry detergent on sale; I figured that if I was going for a miracle, I might as well have it all.) I paid for the items, gracefully returned to my car, and drove calmly through traffic and signal lights back to the post office.

I did not expect the post office to still be open, but it was. I returned to the same window, taped the package, and handed it to the clerk. I looked at the clock—it read *11:58*. I was stunned. There was no logical way I could have done all of that in eight minutes! But I did.

On Monday I phoned my assistant in New Jersey and told her to expect a package sometime during the coming week. "You mean the one that arrived this morning?" she asked.

The package was delivered *Monday morning!* I had sent it via regular mail, not express. Due to time-zone differences, mail traveling from Hawaii to New Jersey *loses* six hours. The package went from my hands to hers in 45 hours, with a weekend in between—faster than the post office's fastest service. Now *that's* a miracle.

When you relax about time, events occur that would otherwise be logistically impossible. Don't try to figure it out. Just watch and enjoy it. While this phenomenon seems like a miracle, it is a perfectly scientific demonstration that mind flexes time.

Chronos and Kairos

In the Greek Bible, the first translation of the Old Testament from the original Aramaic, we find two different words for time. *Chronos* represents time as we know it, dividing our temporal journey into seconds, minutes, hours, days, weeks, months, and years. *Kairos* is a more difficult word to translate, since we do not have one word or a common experience to represent it. The best way to translate *kairos* is "when the time is right," "in the appropriate season," "in the fullness of time," or "in God's time." All of these expressions do not depend on a clock, but on the innate rhythmic wisdom of life.

Our culture lives almost entirely by chronos. Someone asks you, "Are you ready for dinner?" and you look at your watch rather than consulting your stomach. Some couples are so busy that they have to set appointments to make love rather than letting passion move them.

In Japan there is a maxim, "The Christmas cakes are stale on December 26," implying that a woman who is not married by age 25 is too old. Consequently, many young Japanese women are pressured into marriage before they are ready, and they walk a gangplank to years of pain and sorrow. If they trusted kairos more than chronos and married when they were ready, they would maximize their chances for a happy partnership.

We could all use a good dose or kairos. If you flow with life, you will find doors opening that would remain shut under the heavy onus of chronos. Many of us sport chronometers (watches) on our wrists. How different

> For everything there is a season, and a time for every purpose under heaven.
> — Ecclesiastes 3:1

would our lives be if we wore "kairometers," and consulted the natural timing of events rather than a schedule we superimpose with our demands.

Spirit and Time

While some people are procrastinators and put off until to-morrow what they can do today, I find more people who are *pre-crastinators*, trying to jam into today what they can do tomorrow.

If you feel stressed about time, it is not because life, the universe, or God is making undue demands on you. It is because you are making undue demands on yourself. Either (1) you have stacked more items on your to-do list than you can reasonably accomplish; (2) you have set unreasonable deadlines for yourself (the word *deadline* is apt if you kill yourself in the process); (3) others have imposed demands or deadlines on you, and you have accepted them; or (4) you have developed a worry habit that you apply to time.

In my seminars I suggest an affirmation to people who believe they do not have enough time:

> **I always have enough time to do the things
> that my Higher Power would have me do.**

I receive many positive reports from those who use the affirmation, and it will work for you if you apply it when you begin to feel overwhelmed. To deepen its benefits, ask yourself:

> *What is it that I really need to do now, or today,
> and what can I do later (or not at all)?*

If you are honest, you will find that your pressure is usually not situational, but attitudinal. At such a moment you would do well to make the same agreement with yourself that I did at the outset of my tape miracle:

> *I will do whatever I can do with a sense of ease, flow, and
> inner peace; and trust that all will get done. If my task requires any
> sense of struggle, fear, conflict, hurry, or worry, I will not go there.*

If you have been taught that struggle is a requirement for happiness, this sounds like heresy. Yet it may be precisely the statement of sanity you need to hear. Acting with faith in yourself, time, and the universe can transform your day from a frantic chase to an enjoyable current.

Consider the Hawaiian bumper sticker: TRY RELAX. Take back the power you have given to time. Simply trust that you will get done what you need to get done, and the rest is not worth worrying about. Is rushing really worth sacrificing your peace of mind and health? Nothing is more important than feeling good. When you act from inner peace rather than frenzy, you will accomplish positive results in far less time and have some left over to breathe.

> Hurry with your feet, not with your head.
> — Hilda Charlton

My friend Marge was late while driving to an appointment with her therapist, and she got stuck behind a slow driver on a two-lane road. Marge tried and tried to pass the car in front of her, but oncoming traffic would not allow her to do so. As time went on, she became more and more frustrated and upset. Finally she found an opening and floored the accelerator. As Marge passed the slow driver, she turned to look at her nemesis, and saw that it was her therapist! Ultimately there was no need to worry. Marge was already in a synchronistic flow. It was only her mind that told her there was a problem.

There really is no problem with time unless you make one up. Just as you have made up a story that you *don't* have enough time, you can make up a story that you *have* enough time. You cannot stop or turn back the hands of a clock, but you can control your experience of time by repositioning your relationship to it. When you change your mind about time, you transcend time and it cannot control you. You can find enough time, like all things in your life, by choosing a supply mentality. It's not about time. It's about enough.

27

DOCTOR IN
THE HOUSE

If you do not get it from yourself, where will you go for it?

— ATTRIBUTED TO **BUDDHA**

The pharmaceutical industry is one of the largest in the world. In 2009, patients around the globe spent $837 billion on prescription drugs. In the United States, consumers spent $235 billion on prescription drugs, estimated by the U.S. Department of Health and Human Services to increase to $516 billion by 2017. From 1997 to 2007, the number of prescriptions purchased in the U.S. increased 72 percent compared to the population growth of 11 percent, and 2.3 billion drugs were ordered or provided during physician visits in 2008 alone. In 2010, over-the-counter drug sales topped $17 billion. From the years 1995 to 2002, pharmaceutical manufacturing was the nation's most profitable industry, and continues to be one of the biggest moneymakers.

While the use of pharmaceutical, over-the-counter, and illicit drugs is exploding, there is one fact that most doctors, drug manufacturers, and pharmacists, as well as your neighborhood drug dealer, rarely mention: Your body is capable of manufacturing all the drugs you need for healing and well-being. You can live a long, happy, healthy, active life without ever ingesting one synthetic medicinal substance.

I met a fellow who grew up in Hana, the remote area on Maui populated mostly by native Hawaiians and their descendants. He told me that his grandmother had just died at the age of 117. "She never rode in a car, watched television, or saw a doctor," the man reported. Foreign as such a lifestyle might be to those of us who have grown up with technology and medicine, this grandma delivers a striking lesson: *Nature provides.*

When I lived in Fiji, I met many people who were too poor to go to a doctor or who lived too far from a city to get medical treatment. They took full advantage of "leaf medicine," utilizing only plants in the wild to heal themselves. Once while I was trimming a tree, I cut my hand. My Fijian companion walked to a nearby bush, plucked a leaf, and wrapped it around the cut. "This will stop the bleeding and speed healing," he told me. And that it did.

While modern medicines certainly serve us, we would do well to explore medicines directly from nature. Every medicine we need to heal us has been provided through green living things and the minerals embedded in the earth. In many ways modern

> And as I gave you the green plants, I give you everything.
> — Genesis 9:3

medicine is simply reinventing the wheel, with more side effects than the original wheel. Perhaps the Hana grandma offers not just a vision of where we have come from, but where we can return if we choose.

The Closest Drugstore

In recent years biochemists have identified many substances produced within our bodies that create healing, happiness, and euphoria.

Dopamine, for example, is a pleasure hormone secreted by your body when you eat, have sex, have fun, pray, and meditate. Psychiatrists have administered dopamine to patients in catatonic states, with positive, normalizing results (as portrayed in the motion picture *Awakenings*). When you get a cortisone injection for pain relief, that shot is mimicking or substituting for the cortisone your body knows how to produce naturally. Oxytocin, also known as the "love hormone," shows up in your system during orgasm, social recognition, and maternal behaviors, and when petting your dog (your dog gets an oxytocin rush, too!). Biologists have also discovered a substance in the brain called *anandamide,* which induces a state of euphoria for those who use marijuana. The capacity to produce the chemical was already there, simply stimulated by an external substance. Ultimately everything you need to be happy, healthy, and "high" is already within you.

Why, then, are we so addicted to drugs from the store when we can get them for free without leaving home?

1. When we live in ways that run counter to our natural state and we are under physical, mental, and emotional stress, our innate healing systems suffer and atrophy. Toxins from polluted air, water, and food compromise our immune system, and we lose access to our inherent ability to renew ourselves.

2. We are subject to the belief systems of the world we grow up in. At young ages we were taught that pills, injections, machines, and surgery are the answer to what ails us. Doctors are regarded as supreme authority figures, like unto gods, with the magical power to heal us by writing a prescription or piercing our body with tools. Few doctors and

> The art of medicine consists of amusing the patient while nature cures the disease.
> — attributed to Voltaire

patients recognize that *belief is the greater part of healing.* If we believe something will heal us, it will. We believe in drugs, so they heal us. Yet because they are synthetic and chemically distinct from natural healing substances, many drugs have detrimental side effects, some are addictive, and habitual use reinforces the belief that health comes from something outside of us.

In the 1950s, psychologist Dr. Hans Eysenck did a cross-cultural study of healing. He studied patients of doctors practicing many different modalities, including medical doctors, shamans, and faith healers. His results were fascinating. Doctors from all cultures, no matter their method of healing, elicited similar results: one-third of their patients improved, one-third maintained the same health condition they came with, and one-third got worse. The study indicates that no particular form of healing is more effective than another. The source of healing is the belief, expectation, and choice of the patient.

A Course in Miracles (Manual for Teachers) offers an eye-opening statement about who gets healed and how:

> Who is the physician? Only the mind of the patient himself. The outcome is what he decides that it is. Special agents seem to be ministering to him, yet they but give form to his own choice. He chooses them in order to bring tangible form to his desires. And it is this they do, and nothing else. They are not actually needed at all. The patient could merely rise up without their aid and say, "I have no use for this." There is no form of sickness that would not be cured at once.

If you believe in drugs or surgery, they will heal you. If you believe in a diet, acupuncture, herbs, prayer, the laying on of hands, or surgery, *that* will heal you. There is no magic in the potion. The real magic is in the mind.

3. Pharmaceutical companies and doctors who prescribe drugs have a huge investment in people needing drugs. Drug companies are addicted to your addiction to their products. Doctors want and need you to believe in what they offer, and often receive gifts and referral commissions for recommending particular drugs and laboratory tests. Certainly many of these drugs and tests are helpful, but one must take into account the reward system behind use of these methods. If a worldwide headline announced, "You already have all you need to heal yourself," and patients believed and acted on this advice, many doctors and drug companies would be

out of business. It is a rare healer who tells you, as Jesus told one of his patients, "take up your bed, and walk."

I am not suggesting you quit taking drugs or seeing doctors. They can and do help. Allopathic medicine has a role in the universal design for healing. Yet there are other modalities that may be quite effective for those who wish to activate their innate power to heal.

Regenerate

I am fascinated by creatures that can regenerate body parts. If you sever a starfish's limb, it will grow a new one. If you cut an earthworm in half, it will become whole again. In the Caribbean I saw a cat bite off the tail of a lizard. A local fellow told me that soon the lizard would have a new one.

If primitive creatures such as an earthworm, starfish, and lizard can restore their body parts, a far more evolved and infinitely more sophisticated mechanism like the human body should be able to do the same. But it is rarely so. Why? Because we do not believe we can. We do not have models for regeneration, and the medical establishment does not expect it to happen. Yet as spiritual beings, we are not subject simply to the laws and limits of medicine. We are more fundamentally subject to the laws of spirit, which make use of the laws of medicine, but also transcend them.

> I am under no laws but God's.
> — *A Course in Miracles*

Some people glimpse broader possibilities for healing and demonstrate that regeneration is possible. I know a woman who had breast-reduction surgery and applied some herbs on the incisions to promote their healing. She did not realize that these herbs would have an adverse effect, and she developed gangrene in one of her breasts, to the point that it entirely disintegrated. Yet she was determined to regrow her breast, and she did. I've met several people who had a lung removed, and regenerated it. I am acquainted with a fellow who accidentally sliced off half of his thumb with a power saw and restored it. Do these people have special healing powers? No more than you or I. They simply mobilized the power we all possess.

All Healing Is Faith Healing

All healing is accomplished by some form of faith. Everyone believes in something. Drugs and surgery work because we believe in them, so Western medicine is also a form of faith healing. Ultimately it matters less what you have faith in, and more that you simply have faith in something. Even atheists have faith in their belief system. They worship at the altar of no God.

All faith falls into two categories: faith in something outside you, and faith in something inside you. Since everything you see outside you is a projection of your thoughts, all faith ultimately proceeds from something inside you. When I visited the Soviet Union on several citizen-diplomacy missions in the 1980s, our group had a dialogue with Russian citizens on the subject of religion. We had been taught that Communists were godless atheists. When we got to know the people, however, we found that their true beliefs did not reflect the party line of Communism. They told us that they did not believe in God, but they did believe in a power deep within themselves. "We believe in the power with us, too!" some members of our group shared.

Some mysterious Force has created the amazing manifest universe, and you in it. At this moment, life is living through you, beating your heart, breathing your lungs, and orchestrating trillions of infinitely complex microscopic processes every millisecond in all of your organs and systems. The same Force that created you can heal you. Whether you go to an M.D., shaman, herbalist, energy worker, or faith healer, the power to heal is available to you. You don't need to be tired, depressed, or sick. This is not the Creator's will for you, or your will for yourself. There is a doctor in the house, and that physician is with you wherever you go. Look outside for confirmation, but look inside for truth.

28

A BETTER VIEW
OF THE SKY

Now that my house has burnt down,
I have a better view of the sky.

— ZEN PROVERB

During the Japanese earthquake of March 2011, English teacher Anne Thomas was living in Sendai, a severely damaged city near the epicenter of the quake. A few days after the disaster, I received a forwarded e-mail from one of Anne's friends, sharing her gripping yet inspiring view of the difficulties that faced so many.

In the throes of ongoing aftershocks, Anne recounted, everyone was advised to leave their doors open. Yet there was no looting or stealing, and people bonded to support one another. Anne would come home and find someone had left a bag of food at her doorstep. Without utilities, people depended on kerosene heaters. "We sleep lined up in one room, eat by candlelight, and share stories," Anne wrote. "It is warm, friendly, and beautiful." Without water, people could not bathe or shower. Yet Anne saw a blessing even in this: "We feel grubby, but there are more important concerns than that for us now. I love this peeling away of non-essentials.

Living fully on the level of instinct, of intuition, of caring, of what is needed for survival, not just of me, but of the entire group."

When a household had running water, the owner posted signs so others could come and fill up their buckets. "People keep saying, 'This is how it used to be in the old days when everyone helped one another.'"

Anne poetically described her transformed environment: "The heavens at night are scattered with stars. I usually can see about two, but now the whole sky is filled." (Her observation reminded me of a group of Japanese visitors who attended one of my retreats in Hawaii. The most common comment I heard was: "We didn't know there were so many stars! We have so many city lights that we never see them.")

Anne Thomas concluded: "An enormous Cosmic evolutionary step is occurring all over the world. . . . I can feel my heart opening very wide. . . . I feel part of something happening much larger than myself. This wave of birthing worldwide is hard, and yet magnificent."

Anne's letter eloquently illuminates that awakening, transformation, and healing can come out of devastation. Beauty and values were revealed by the disaster that were formerly obscured by busyness, fear, and technology. Could the earthquake and other shake-ups, physical, emotional, and societal, be offering us course corrections to help us get back on track with our true nature and how we were born to live?

The High Art of Reframing

When you shift perspective, you shift results. *Reframing* is the technique of taking the facts of a troubling situation and finding another way to see them that is empowering. Everything that happens

> If you fall in a mud puddle, check your pockets for fish.
> — Source unknown

is simply data, information. The meaning it has depends on the meaning you project onto it. You can spin any fact for or against you, so why not spin it in your favor?

Here are some examples of practical reframes:

> After the great Argentinean golfer Roberto De Vicenzo won a tournament, he received his prize check and left the clubhouse. As the champion walked to his car in the parking lot, he was approached by a young woman. She congratulated him on his victory and told him that her child was seriously ill and near death. She did not know how she could pay the doctor's bills and hospital expenses.
>
> De Vicenzo was touched by her story, so he took out a pen and endorsed his winning check for payment to the woman. "Make some good days for the baby," he said as he pressed the check into her hand.
>
> The next week De Vicenzo was having lunch in a country club when a Professional Golfers Association official came to his table. "Some of the boys told me you met a young woman in the parking lot last week after you won that tournament."
>
> De Vicenzo nodded.
>
> "Well," said the official, "I have news for you. She's a phony. She has no sick baby. She's not even married. She fleeced you, my friend."
>
> "You mean there is no baby who is dying?" asked De Vicenzo.
>
> "That's right," said the official.
>
> "That's the best news I've heard all week," De Vicenzo answered.
>
> — from *The Best of Bits & Pieces*

When Chikako was in kindergarten, her teacher instructed the students to draw pictures of their mothers as a gift for Mother's Day. Chikako told her mother about the drawing, and she was very pleased. "I'm looking forward to seeing it!" she told her daughter.

The teacher posted all the students' pictures on the classroom bulletin board. On the last school day before Mother's Day, the students were asked to take their pictures off the bulletin board and bring them home to their mothers.

When Chikako reached the bulletin board, she found that someone had taken the picture she had drawn. An inquiry proved unable to locate the lost drawing, so Chikako had the unpleasant duty to tell her mother that the picture she had lovingly created had been stolen. Terrified, Chikako made the report.

But instead of the scolding Chikako expected, her mother smiled and told her, "That must have been a really beautiful picture if someone else wanted it enough to take it. You must be a great artist!"

A young Kansas City artist, struggling to realize his dream of drawing cartoons for a living, was turned away from every newspaper he approached for a job. "Forget it," editors told him. "You have no talent. Find yourself another career." Rejection followed rejection, until one day he found himself holed up in a dilapidated, mice-infested garage, hopeless and penniless.

Having plenty of time on his hands, the artist began to sketch the mice running across the windowsill above his desk. Fascinated with the little creatures, he developed a friendly relationship with one tiny fellow, and focused his drawings on him.

Little did the man realize how important this relationship would be for him. The artist's name was Walt Disney. The mouse's name turned out to be "Mickey," and Walt and Mickey went on to become two of the most successful entertainers in the world, bringing happiness and joy to countless children and families.

Events are more like putty than rocks. You can mold all experiences in your favor if you so choose. The more you practice reframing, the more joy you will experience, and the more positive results you will beget.

Positive Disintegration

Sometimes when we hit bottom, we bounce back higher than if we had not taken a journey to the netherworld. The energy generated by plummeting becomes fuel for transformation. Many people have risen to greatness as a result of personal hardship because the experience motivated

> I have no money, no resources, no hopes. I am the happiest man alive.
> — Henry Miller

them to chart a new course for their lives. They were not destroyed by their challenge, but empowered by it.

In his book *Positive Disintegration,* psychiatrist Dr. Kazimierz Dabrowski recounts his experience working with patients at a mental institution. Dabrowski discovered that their worlds had crashed because their lives had become overwhelming and unmanageable. The only way for them to cope was to let everything fall apart. Only then could their lives come together in a new and healthier way. So their nervous breakdown was really a nervous *breakthrough.*

Often you must break down before you can break through. In this sense, disintegrate becomes *disintegreat* and leads to you being *disintegrateful.*

If your life isn't working, partially or wholly, it will not help to just keep plugging along or numb yourself with alcohol, drugs, work, busyness, shopping, sex, the Internet, gossip, or inane television. Your pain is a wake-up call. Tell the truth about what hurts so you can heal it. Pain becomes chronic only when you are willing to put up with it. Situations are not painful; how you respond to them is. Choose a different response and you become *response-able*, or responsible. Then your life belongs to you.

If something wants or needs to fall apart, or does so beyond your ability to control, *let it.* Life is supposed to work well, and you are supposed to be happy in it. If a relationship or institution is dysfunctional, the best thing that can happen is for it to disintegrate. When it does, thank God. You are being saved from continuing in a situation that was hurting you. Now the door is open for something better. Walk through that door and claim what awaits.

Wise Creations

If you have read any self-help book, attended a seminar, or been the client of a coach or counselor, you have likely heard the expression "How did you create that?" While the principle of personal responsibility for creation is true, the question is usually misused by asking it at the wrong time and in the wrong way. If you've just fallen out of a tree and broken your arm and you are lying in pain, and your self-help friend comes along and asks you, "How did you create that?" you might likely use your remaining arm to punch that person and then ask, "And how did you create *that?*"

The time to remind people that they are the creators of their experiences is not when they are in pain. At such a moment they need compassion, kindness, support to heal, and action toward resolution. In this situation love is far more effective than introspection. After people feel better and are in a position to assess the dynamics of their mishap, they can more readily accept responsibility for their role in the misfortune and look for ways to keep it from it happening again.

Usually when someone asks you, "How did you create that?" the question contains an implicit ". . . you idiot." Read between the lines: "That was a really stupid move. I sure hope you learn your lesson so you don't screw up again." The speaker might imply this judgment in his or her question, or you may simply read judgment into it. One way or another it is there.

There is another spin on "How did you create that?" that works a lot better. Insert the words *in wisdom* in the question, so it becomes "How *in wisdom* did you create that?" How did you draw that experience to you because you knew it would serve you and the others involved? What part of you took that on as a highly useful element in your awakening? What was brilliant about that move? How do you deserve credit for setting up a lesson that would improve your life?

Now that feels a lot better than *"You dummkopf!"*—doesn't it?

No matter how gnarly a situation appears, you are always creating in favor of your advancement. Often the screwups contribute to your growth more than the routine ride. In the big picture, you can't really get it wrong. If you have learned, the experience has served.

⌐

Change is inevitable and, as the colloquial phrase goes, "shit happens." Yet it is even truer that *shift* happens. You may not be able to control events, but you can control attitude and response to events. Perhaps universities of the future, more metaphysically based, will confer M.A. degrees—Master of Attitude. Then you might go on to get your M.B.U., and become a Mobile Blessing Unit.

Even apparent disasters can serve as an element of enoughness in your life. I am not belittling difficulties or encouraging them. I am inviting you to take what appears to be misfortune on one level, and find fortune in it on another level. Fortune is not a fact; it is an interpretation. Every minus is a half of a plus waiting for a stroke of vertical awareness. As you learn to interpret experiences in your favor, they work more and more in your favor. Then when anyone asks you, "How did you create that?" or "How could life send that experience your way?" your answer will be: "In utter brilliance."

29

NOT GONNA TAKE
IT ANYMORE

*Some people change when they see the light,
others when they feel the heat.*

— ATTRIBUTED TO **CAROLINE SCHOEDER**

In a classic scene in the movie *Network,* irate television news broadcaster Howard Beale sticks his head out of his Manhattan office window and screams that he's mad as hell and he's not going to take it anymore. During his next broadcast, Beale encourages all viewers who are fed up to do the same. Soon we see people across the nation throwing open their windows and shouting that they, too, are mad as hell and they're not going to take it anymore.

You may be surprised that a book on contentment would glorify such an outburst of rage. Yet putting your foot down is the first step to moving ahead. I have heard countless testimonies from people who went along with distasteful situations for many years because they did not want to rock the boat. But if the boat is sinking, you cannot afford to stay in it. Drowning in unhappiness is not an expression of contentment. That is complacency.

When you put up with situations that stifle, insult, or abuse you over a length of time, you can entirely shift the pattern by shouting to the universe, *"I refuse to put up with this any longer!"* In that instant, you end malaise as a way of life and turn your ship from desperation toward possibility.

We learn by contrast. One of the ways we get clear on who we are, what we want, and where we belong, is to become disgusted with living in ways that don't work.

> Dismiss whatever insults your own soul.
> — Walt Whitman

Sometimes your soul needs to get rashly insulted before you take measures to uplift it. If you have gotten to that point, your time in Hades has not been wasted; it has catapulted you toward the Elysian fields.

Defining Moments

"My 21-year-old daughter is driving me crazy," Alice reported in a seminar. "She hasn't been able to hold a job, so she lives with me. Her drug-addled boyfriend stays over, and when I come home, the apartment reeks of pot. Her dog poops all over the place, and she doesn't clean it up. She throws tantrums and locks me out of the bathroom."

"Why don't you ask her to leave?" I had to ask.

Alice squeezed her brow and replied, "I would feel guilty about being a bad mother."

I told Alice that her guilt was not helping her or her daughter. Instead, some well-placed boundaries would give her respite and motivate her daughter to step into adult shoes. Alice agreed to do a role-playing exercise in which she told her daughter that she needed to respect the rules of her mother's house, or she would have to move out.

Over several rounds of the role play, Alice found confidence to lay down the law to her daughter, and her communication gained genuine authority. Her statement became so powerful that the audience gave her a standing ovation.

Several months later I received an e-mail from Alice telling me that she had set strong boundaries with her daughter, prohibiting drug use in her house and requiring her daughter to clean up after her dog and leave the bathroom unlocked. The daughter made a fuss and moved out for a while, but later returned on the condition she would comply with her mother's terms.

"Our relationship is transformed," Alice wrote. "We're still working some things out, but now I actually enjoy living in my own home. My daughter demonstrates more maturity, and I feel closer to her. The conversation in which I set boundaries was the turning point."

⌒

We all have defining moments when we are required to make a stand for what we believe, want, and deserve.

If you capture that moment and use it on your behalf, your life will change. If you let the moment pass without acting, painful situations continue, and you delay your liberation until you finally decide to take effective action.

> If you don't stand for something, you'll fall for anything.
> — Source unknown

Sometimes defining moments show up in the form of an accident, divorce, emotional blowup, financial crash, legal issue, illness, or other "in-your-face" scenario. But you don't have to wait until you get to the edge of the cliff (or are hanging over it) before you make powerful, self-affirming decisions. Life comes to drama only when you do not heed the more subtle signs.

If something you are doing is strangling your soul, use your frustration, upset, or anger as fuel to energize your next step. Don't dwell on who or what is wrong, but as soon as you realize what is *not it,* use that awareness to identify what is *it* and then move full speed ahead toward higher ground. In this way all situations serve, and a challenge transforms into a stepping-stone to something better.

Dynamic Contentment

Contentment is not a stagnant pool, but a dynamic stream that keeps you moving in new and often unexpected directions. Following the current of excitement will take you to more fascinating and rewarding places than clinging to known rocks. If you do not flow with your joy, you will stagnate and die, emotionally and possibly physically. People die when: (1) the passion in their lives dwindles to a tiny spark—or nothing—and they have nothing left to live for; or (2) they have fanned the flame of their passion to the max, done all they wish to do, and are ready to go home with joy and satisfaction for their earthly journey.

> I want to be thoroughly used up when I die. . . . Life is no "brief candle" for me. It is a sort of splendid torch, which I have got hold of for the moment; and I want to make it burn as brightly as possible before handing it on to future generations.
> — George Bernard Shaw

My friend Cindy's marriage had dwindled to the barest flicker of its original flame. She and her husband had grown in different directions; more accurately, she had grown and changed, but her husband was essentially the same man of 20 years previous. The couple shared few common activities, they had no emotional connection, and their sexual relationship was nil. Cindy was just waiting for her teenage son and daughter to graduate from high school and leave the nest so she could get a divorce. "My friends tell me to have an affair," Cindy told me. "But I wouldn't do that. I have integrity."

Not really. Integrity means that the life you are living in the outer world is an expression of your inner truth. I respected Cindy for not cheating on her husband, but by staying in a loveless situation, she was cheating herself.

I am not suggesting that Cindy have a love affair with another man. I am suggesting, rather, that she have a love affair with herself and do whatever it takes to keep her joy alive.

Possible solutions:

- Cindy might let her husband know of her unhappiness and initiate a conversation to open up communication and deepen their connection.

- She and her husband might go to counseling and seek to renew their relationship.

- Cindy might move ahead with a divorce and trust that her children would do fine or be even better off for not watching their parents die in their relationship.

- She might choose to stay married until the kids leave, and meanwhile do everything she can to nourish her soul even if it is not finding fulfillment in her marriage.

When you get clear on your intention, all kinds of options open up to you that you cannot see when your intention is muddy. There is always a path available in alignment with your integrity if you are willing to seek and live it.

The Source of Real Change

When you decide that you are mad as hell and you refuse to take it anymore, you may be tempted to gather a posse and lynch all the troublemakers. Yet other people are not the source of your angst. Something inside you is agreeing with the adverse situation and continuing to choose it.

> Every doormat says "Welcome."
> — Source unknown

If you feel stuck in a situation that seems beyond your control, ask yourself, "What is my payoff in allowing the situation to continue?" There is something you are getting out of staying in your current position. Usually the payoff is a sense of safety in the known, control over your world, numbing or distraction from pain, or reinforcement for a victim position. If you can be honest about why you might be choosing your situation, recognize

209

that the *perceived* reward is not a *real* reward, and consider what greater reward you would receive from changing, you tip the balance toward freedom. Despite appearances, you are the director of your movie.

If you "lynch" anyone or anything, let it be the part of your mind that believes you need to compromise your happiness. When you withdraw your agreement that a toxic situation is acceptable, you deactivate the magnet that has kept it in force. Then you will either upgrade the current situation to one that works better for you, or you will leave with dignity—or the other person will leave. Or your grievance may simply dissolve. It matters less *how* the change occurs, and more that you recognize that change is necessary. Then the Law of Attraction will help you orchestrate the details.

Sometimes your desired change will happen through you, and sometimes it will happen around you. Are you doing everything you can do on your own behalf? If so, you have done your part, and your job is to hold the situation in positive vision and trust that universal forces will support your intentions. If you have not taken all possible action you can, take the next step you can from a base of clarity, vision, and inner peace.

Protracted anger will only impede your progress. You can be fed up with a situation and move full speed ahead to change it without any engaging in a battle mentality. The real fight is within yourself—the same place that true peace can be found. When you do your spiritual homework, you will receive helping hands in wondrous and sometimes miraculous ways.

Love How Much You Hate It

The admission that you find something detestable and you will no longer participate in it can be one of the most liberating moments of your life. At such a moment, you get excited about replacing the undesirable behavior or situation with a new one that makes your life far better. At that point the pain that accompanies compromise will become your friend, urging you sharply to move out of it. "Pain pushes and vision pulls."

When I work with a client who has discovered an unwanted habit and deeply desires to change it, I say, "I am going to give you a posthypnotic suggestion: the next time you ____ [start to accept a date with someone you don't like] [fight with your spouse over a petty subject] [go to work on a vacation day], your tongue will start to burn, or your body will become so stiff that you can't continue."

Of course I am kidding, but there is a valid principle behind my intention: I hope and pray that what rubs you the wrong way will become so obnoxious to you that you will choose to do what brings you joy instead.

No one should have to put up with any situation that is demeaning or deadening. Demand of God that you discover the lesson that will free you, and do not let God off the hook until It delivers. Your soul has chosen difficult experiences for reasons your mind could not fathom—

> All journeys have secret destinations of which the traveler is unaware.
> — Martin Buber

until now. Use the experiences to activate the power within you, and the situation will transform from a curse to a blessing. The devil foe will become an angel ally. Then you will realize this had to happen for the benefit of your awakening. Mad as hell leads to glad as heaven.

*The present is saturated with the past
and pregnant with the future.*

— ATTRIBUTED TO **GOTTFRIED WILHELM LEIBNIZ**

30

CONTENT TO WANT MORE

Happy and hungry. It's a healthy formula for a successful life.

— ANTHONY ROBBINS

In coaching, Ginny told me that she was dissatisfied with her relationship with her boyfriend. "I want to have more . . . you know," she reported.

"'You know'?" I tried to get her to clarify.

Ginny began to squirm and fidget. "You know . . ." she repeated.

"Do you mean sex?"

"Uh-huh." She giggled.

"Why do you have such a hard time saying the word *sex*?" I had to ask.

"I grew up in a church that told me that it's evil and sinful to want sex. Especially for a woman."

"Have you ever told your boyfriend that you would like more sex?" I asked.

"Oh no!" Ginny replied. "I could never do that!"

Thus our coaching journey began, along with the transformation of Ginny's relationship.

Some churches and philosophies teach that desire is bad, and you should not want anything. The key to peace, they advise, is to rid yourself of desire. Yet ridding yourself of desire is impossible, since the propensity to expand, deepen, and grow is built into the fabric of creation. Even if you meditate or do spiritual practices to get rid of desire, you are desiring peace. So we might as well just accept that desire happens, and work its dynamic power to our advantage rather than trying to exorcise it.

> Life in Lubbock, Texas, taught me two things: One is that God loves you and you're going to burn in hell. The other is that sex is the most awful, filthy thing on earth and you should save it for someone you love.
> — Butch Hancock

One of my favorite movies, *Dangerous Beauty,* is based on the true story of Veronica Franco, a courtesan of 16th-century Venice. Veronica was a favorite among Venetian statesmen, not simply on account of her sexual favors but because she was a radiant spirit. Unlike other Venetian women of her era, she had obtained an education, which made her the intellectual equal of her male associates. In an odd way, she was a healer, bringing vision, exuberance, and a keen mind to her profession and her life.

When the Inquisition arrived in Venice, Veronica was accused of being a witch and beguiling men. Brought to trial, she faced execution unless she confessed to being a witch. In the movie's stirring courtroom speech, Veronica boldly confessed. But not to the charges as stated. She confessed that she found more ecstasy in passion than in prayer. To her, passion *was* prayer.

I am not suggesting you become a courtesan (unless that is your true calling). I *am* suggesting that you regard passion as a force for good in your life. Passion is not the work of the devil, unless it is misunderstood and misused. Passion is an expression of God, the universe's way of guiding you to be in your right place at the right time with the right people for the right purpose. While passion can be misdirected, it can also propel you to fulfill your destiny and bring you deep satisfaction as you uplift humanity.

Passion is not a denial of God; it is the primary avenue through which God gives life.

Ask with Confidence

While you may have been taught that asking for what you want is selfish, it is far more selfish to live in denial of what you want. When you stifle your passion, you become dispirited, irritable, and nonproductive. Broadcasting the frequency of despair sucks energy from the people around you. Surfing on the cutting

> Ask for 100% of what you want 100% of the time.
> — Stan Dale

edge of your joy invites them to ride the wave with you. Your real contribution to life is how you feel. The better you feel, the more you have to offer.

The most powerful form of asking is to ask without demanding. Voice your desire without attachment to fulfillment in the way you envision it. If this sounds paradoxical, it is. You have to simultaneously ask and trust that if something is right for you, you will receive it without having to fuss and fight for it. If it becomes a struggle, it's not "it." There may be something even better for you. If so, it will come, and you will be glad you received that instead of what you originally wanted.

Buddha taught nonattachment, not nondesire. He realized that desire happens. Suffering is caused by attachment to desire. The thought *I would like that* is natural. The idea *I will throw a tantrum if I don't get it* is what gets you into trouble. Do you trust that the hand of love will take care of you and you will be provided for even if you don't struggle and strain to get what you want? There is a huge difference between calm, focused, steady action and feverish manipulation.

Attachment bounces you up and down on the roller coaster of external conditions: the stock market rises and you feel rich; it falls and you feel poor . . . your honey says, "I love you" and you are exuberant; he ignores you and you are crushed . . . you see a movie with a happy ending and you feel warm and fuzzy; you watch the news and you get depressed. In all of these situations, you allow your peace to depend on something outside you. Meanwhile there is a place inside you that is capable of feeling good no matter what the stock market, your lover, or the news is doing. That is the place to establish your spiritual residence.

Finding Your Just-Right Tribe

If you are not happy where you are, perhaps you are being called elsewhere.

Ever since Dana was a child, her family had groomed her to go into the field of medicine. Her father was a doctor, as was his father, her brother, and several other relatives. At a young age, Dana simply accepted the medical profession as her destiny and went along with all the preparations her family made for her to follow that course.

Dana went to medical school, got her M.D., and went into practice at a large hospital in her city. At first she felt satisfied, partly because she was helping people, but mostly because she had finally fulfilled the demands her family had imposed upon her for her entire life.

After a few years, Dana became disenchanted with the medical profession. The required paperwork was a huge burden and distraction from personal contact with her patients, and the cloud of fear that hung over the industry due to hyper-regulation was enormous. But mostly Dana believed that modern medicine reduced human beings to a collection of unrelated organs, and most treatments were about damage control rather than helping people to live healthy lives by taking good care of themselves.

When Dana heard about a trip to China for doctors, something inside her moved her to attend. On the tour she was introduced to healing practices that treated people as whole and recognized the presence of *chi,* or life force, that Western medicine seemed unaware of. Dana felt as if she was coming home to something profound that she always knew existed, but did not have a way to get to. But now she did.

Upon returning to the America, Dana took courses in acupuncture, herbology, and tai chi chuan. These classes inspired her far more than Western medicine ever had. Eventually she got a degree in Chinese medicine and planned to quit her job in the hospital and open a private acupuncture clinic.

You can imagine the resistance Dana encountered from her family, who called her a kook and told her that she would be an embarrassment to the family's long and respected medical tradition. Dana wrestled with the decision, but her affinity for Asian healing was so strong that she could not deny it, and she chose to follow this course.

Dana's healing practice became a huge success. There she discovered many people more open to alternative healing than she had imagined. Plus she enjoyed the company of colleagues—her just-right tribe—who shared her values.

One day Dana's father came to her to treat him for recurring migraine headaches that all of his training and techniques could not alleviate. After a few treatments, her dad felt better for the first time in a long time. He told his daughter, "I am so glad that you followed your path."

You, too, have a just-right tribe and a just-right place in life. When you find it, you know it. Until then, you feel a certain malaise. Such discomfort is not a bad thing; divine discontent is prodding you to keep moving ahead.

When eagles build a nest, they construct its foundation with thorny, sharp-edged twigs and branches. Then the parents line the nest with soft, fluffy materials. When the eaglets are first born, they are buffered by the cushy nest. As they get older and thrash about more, they dislodge the cushioning and expose the thorny branches. At that point the nest becomes extremely uncomfortable for them to stay in. They are motivated to fly and claim dominion of the skies. The thorns were not the eaglets' enemy, but their friends.

If something you are doing is growing more and more uncomfortable, perhaps you are being motivated to fly. Staying will only feel worse. I am not suggesting you run away. You must remain in situations until you get clear about why they have shown up and what you need to learn from them. When the time comes to graduate, you need not feel guilty. As the mature eagle spreads its wings and soars over the mountains and valleys below, it feels not a stitch of remorse. It is fulfilling its destiny, as you must fulfill yours.

Preferences Bring Color and Life

I am wary of people who say they have no preferences. If you didn't care one way or the other, you wouldn't be alive. To be alive is to prefer. To prefer without being attached is to be even more alive.

When I ask someone a question about what he would like to do and he answers, "Whatever," "I'll go with the flow," "I'm easy," or "You decide," I miss hearing a real choice. I want to know who that person is and what would make him happy. If you don't tell me who you are and what you want or need, I am at a loss as to how to know you, connect with you, or help you. When you tell me what you want, what you like, how you feel, and what your vision is, I can meet you at a soul level—the level that really matters.

> I was afraid to say "no" because I feared that I would lose my friends. But then I realized that I didn't have any friends because no one knew who I was.
> — Source unknown

One day I gave a talk at a church on the theme "Ask for what you really want." During the break between services, I sat in the minister's office with the minister's assistant Marnie, who asked me which kind of tea I would like. I told her, "Chamomile."

As Marnie searched through the pantry cabinet, she mumbled, "I'm not seeing that at the moment."

Immediately I replied, "That's okay. I'll take whatever you have."

Marnie turned and asked me, "Now are you the same Alan Cohen who just told a large group to not settle for less than what you really want?"

Busted. Marnie resumed her search and came up with a box of chamomile tea. The incident reminded me that I am often quick to say, "Whatever." There is a difference between saying "Whatever" before you try and saying "Whatever" after you try.

In graduate school, I took a group-dynamics course with an eccentric professor who was obsessed with truth telling. During one group session, he asked me who I thought was the most attractive woman in the group. Wanting to be diplomatic, I answered, "I think all the women in the group are attractive."

The professor made a face and told me, "Boy, are you full of it!"

I don't regret my decision to be diplomatic, but I learned from that incident that I do have preferences. There was one woman in the group whom I found especially attractive. Perhaps it would not have been appropriate for me to single her out in public, but it was important for me to acknowledge to myself that I had a preference.

It's not always necessary for you to speak or demand your preferences, but it is necessary for you to know them. Otherwise you become bland and disheartened. If you are bored, you are boring. When you forgo stating your preferences over a long period of time, you lose touch with them. Then you lose your joy and your voice.

When a coaching client stated that she could not decide whether or not to sell her house, I ran her through a series of rapid-fire questions: "What's your favorite color? Ice-cream flavor? Movie? Vacation spot? Sport?" When she was on a roll of honesty about her passion, I asked her, "Do you want to sell your house?"

"Yes, I do!" she stated spontaneously and emphatically, followed by a huge smile. When I had nudged her into the experience of being in touch with her passion in the domains of which she was aware, she gained access to the domains in which she was not aware.

Passion and truth are like muscles: The more you use them, the greater your power to express them. The less you use them, the more they atrophy. That's why it's important to be honest about your preferences.

Sure, there are some things that you really don't care about. But there are other things you do care about. Take care that a habit of saying "I don't care" does not impede your ability to speak your truth when you need to.

What You Really Want

If you have ever feared or battled against wanting something, trust that your desire for more is an intrinsic element in your journey. Yet be not deceived that that thing you want is *really* what you want. What you really want is the experience that the thing represents. It's not money you really want; it's the freedom the money stands for. It's not a mate you really want; it's the love and intimacy you expect will come through a partner. It's not a home you really want; it's the sense of safety, beauty, or serenity a home offers.

Continue to pursue what you want, meanwhile asking, "What do I really want?" Then pursue the experience of freedom, love, and security, or whatever else you desire, right where you stand.

You can be both happy and hungry. Embrace what you own *and* what you want. The devil did not create desire. The devil only created fear of it. Live, act, desire, choose, and achieve in the world, but remember that who you are is far greater than anything you could get. Then the world will become the field upon which you discover that no matter what game you are playing, you have already won.

Do not let your fire go out, spark by irreplaceable spark, in the hopeless swamps of the approximate, the not-quite, the not-yet, the not-at-all. Do not let the hero in your soul perish, in lonely frustration for the life you deserved, but have never been able to reach. Check your road and the nature of your battle. The world you desire can be won, it exists, it is real, it is possible, it is yours.

— **AYN RAND**

31

WHEN ARE
YOU DONE?

On the day you die, you will have e-mail in your in-box.
Then what will you do?

— ROBERT HOLDEN

Sometimes I feel like the Greek mythological figure Sisyphus, who spent eternity pushing a boulder to the top of a hill, only to have it roll back down again. Just as I'm getting up from the computer, an e-mail comes in requiring attention. As soon as I finish weeding at the end of a hedgerow, I notice new weeds sprouting back at the beginning. The car emerges from the car wash all sparkly and runs through a mud puddle. And . . .

The world gives us many prescriptions for what will make us feel complete. If you can just drop those ten stubborn pounds, pay off the credit cards, or find Mr. Right, you will be there. But "there" turns out to be a moving target. Like the goat pulling the cart in hopes of getting a bite of the carrot dangling just beyond its reach, every now and then you get a nibble, but a moment later the carrot moves inches ahead, egging you on to keep pulling.

The problem with goals for completion that the world prescribes is that the rules keep changing. When I was growing up, my Catholic friends were not permitted to eat meat on Fridays because that was a sin. Then one day a group of men had a meeting and announced that God has no problem with Friday meat eating. At some point you have to scratch your head and wonder, *Why am I hustling and sweating for goals and rewards that others set for me?*—especially ones you can never fully attain.

If you are tired of pushing your rock up the hill, take heart. Even while you tread your human journey in quest of completion, you are on a spiritual journey on which you are whole no matter what happens around you. To win the completion game, shift your focus from the part of you that feels incomplete to the part of you that already is complete. You've seen movies in which the camera shifts focus from an actor to the scene behind the actor. Suddenly the actor is a blur and the scenery is sharp. The camera did not move at all; it just changed what it was paying attention to. Likewise you can swing from a sense of lack to a sense of wholeness with but a tweak of your consciousness. Same scene, different angle, entirely different result. You are never more than a thought away from peace.

To find completion, you do not have to sit in a cave for the rest of your life contemplating your navel. Truth be told, a new iPhone gets your juices flowing more than a loincloth. You can be active in the world, doing and achieving, remembering all the while that you are and have enough. The difference is *perspective*.

When you recognize that completion is a choice, not an event, you may continue to do many of the same things you did, but inside you feel different. Your relationship or business is no longer a life-or-death drama, you keep going to the gym, and "the slings and arrows of outrageous fortune" do not rock your world. Your life ceases to be a problem to be solved, and becomes an adventure to be enjoyed.

Some people fear that if they felt complete, their lives would be over and they would be ready for the scrap heap. To the contrary, completion means you enter more fully into life. When you proceed from fullness, you become more present and your actions take on greater power and meaning. Here again we touch paradox, your position of greatest strength: the less you believe you *have* to do, the more you achieve what you *need* to do.

Who Completes You?

The *Jerry Maguire* idea that "you complete me" is romantic but delusional. No one can complete you because you are already complete. If someone can complete you, he or she can empty you. This banal drama forms a substantial plot for countless dysfunctional love songs, movies, and novels, but it is not a worthy story line for anyone who values true love. If you are ready for your life to move beyond a soap opera, claim enoughness that does not depend on a lover's actions.

A healthier way to acknowledge someone you love would be to say, "In your presence, I remember I am whole." With that statement you acknowledge the gift that a beloved brings you, but you retain the power and identity of your intact self.

You do not need anyone to fill you up. You cannot make fuller that which is already full. The best lovers do not leave you feeling empty, but restore your memory that you are eternally full.

When Practice Becomes Perfect

The ego, or limited sense of self, tries to keep you from moving ahead by telling you that you are not ready to do what you want to do. It argues that you are too young, old, poor, inexperienced, unskilled, stupid, out of shape, or laden with dark history . . . or that you need more time, education, money, guidance, support, beauty, or confidence before you can make your move.

When Bryce Courtenay, author of the best-selling novel *The Power of One,* wrote his tome, he considered it his "practice novel," hoping that one day he would develop the skill to pen a really good story. A friend suggested to Bryce that he show his manuscript to an agent, which he did, apologizing that the book was just a warm-up. The agent loved the book and pitched it to a publisher. Before long *The Power of One* became an international bestseller, the most successful book ever to come out of Australia, and the basis for a major motion picture. "I couldn't imagine why all these people were reading my practice novel!" Bryce confessed.

Like Bryce Courtenay, you may be better prepared than you realize. You may think that there are all kinds of prerequisites and

> Don't wait until conditions are perfect to begin. Beginning makes conditions perfect.
> — Howard Cohen

hoops you need to jump through, while the success you seek may be available to you now. You learn to do things well by doing them. If people had to become perfect parents before they could have children, there would be no children! To be a writer, write; to be a singer, sing; to be a dancer, dance. Preparation is important, but do not postpone living your dream because you are eternally getting ready to live your dream.

If It Helps One Person

A publisher asked me to make an audio recording of one of my books. I went into a studio, recorded an abridged form of the book, and submitted it to the publisher. As I handed it to him, I told him, "I don't really like the sound of my voice on the recording."

He smiled and replied, "If this recording helps one person, it's worth offering to the world." His statement pierced my judgments and resonated inside my heart. I had been caught up in the surface level of the production, but the deeper purpose was to inspire and heal. Since that time whenever I have a doubt or misgiving about offering a book, CD, or program, I remember that if the offering makes someone's life better, it is all worth it.

When one of my early books, *Joy Is My Compass*, went out of print due to low sales volume, I began to wonder if it was worth the work to put that book together. Then one evening at a seminar a participant told me, "I read your book *Joy Is My Compass,* and as a result I was inspired to establish an AIDS hospice. Since that time my staff and I have attended to the needs of many AIDS patients who have been scorned and abandoned by their friends and family. Some of them had no one in the world to care for them. Thanks to you, these people have died in dignity in an atmosphere of love, compassion, and caring."

Upon hearing that account, I realized that if nothing else good ever came from me writing that book, that one result would certainly be worth any and all effort I put into it. You have no idea how any of your words, acts, or creations may ripple out into the universe and improve the lives of one person or many, or the entire planet. Just launch your creations and trust God to dispatch them where they can help most. Works or acts that you might judge as less than perfect or that do not create professional success may serve in ways far more profound and healing than some products that land on a chart but leave the soul starving.

A Course in Miracles tells us, "A miracle is never lost. It may touch many people you have not even met, and produce undreamed of changes in situations of which you are not even aware." For this reason, you cannot and must not judge your creations as incomplete because they are not finished or perfect. If you help one person, your work is perfect. (And if that person is you, it is worth it even more!)

You Cannot Be More of What You Already Are

I have discovered a fascinating pattern with my coaching clients: Most people believe that they are not enough of what they already are. An unusually kind client named Anna told me, "I could be more thoughtful to others."

I had to laugh. "I am amazed you are saying that," I replied. "You are one of the most thoughtful people I have ever met."

Yet Anna did not see it. "I am afraid I will become arrogant," she confessed.

I told her, "You have a long, long way to go before you become arrogant." People who worry about being arrogant are in the least danger of it. Arrogant people never worry about being arrogant, although they should. Only humble people are concerned about getting an ego, while they could probably use more of one.

Since that time I have observed this motif played out in many people. Successful entrepreneurs believe they have not yet arrived; bodybuilders think they should be in better shape; home owners with the nicest lawns envy their neighbors' landscaping. And on and on . . .

Consider what you are worried that you are not enough of: Are you not smart enough? Attractive enough? Successful enough in business? A wise enough parent or teacher? A convincing sales-person or public speaker? Then consider that you may already be good at what you think you are not enough of. Maybe *really* good. You are concerned about a particular dimension because that arena is really important to you. What you value, you already are—or you become. Give yourself credit for the gifts and talents you already embody. You are probably further along than you realize.

Which Voice to Heed

Over time I have identified a troublesome voice inside my head, just below the threshold of my awareness. It's more of a feeling than a voice. If I could put words to it, it said something like, *There must be something you have to do that you are forgetting. Some bill to pay, some tax form to submit, someone to call, some appointment to keep, some deadline to meet, some travel to book, something that, if neglected, you will really be sorry.*

Those are just the logistical threats that niggling voice came up with. If I could not find some task I overlooked, the voice moved into spiritual and moral chiding: *You should be meditating more, praying more, doing nicer things for others, exercising, eating better, and making sure you don't waste your life.*

Does this voice or one like it sound familiar to you? It's really a nasty bugger. After listening to it for many years, I came to recognize it for what it really is: fear and illusion. A part of my mind found weird value in worrying, obsessing over past or possible errors and projecting to future problems. When I began to recognize the voice for what it was, its power over me began to diminish. Once in a while it still shows up, but I dismiss it as soon as possible after I identify it. Illusions cannot live in the face of truth.

The voice that tells you that you are not doing enough or you are not enough will never be satisfied. It is radio station KSMOG broadcasting at a specific frequency. To end its mindless rant, switch to another station at a different frequency. KWIN is simultaneously broadcasting, offering infinitely more satisfaction and success. It beams on the wavelength of self-acceptance, self-respect, appreciation, and worthiness. The KWIN voice speaks far more truth to you than KSMOG. Establish your preset buttons and press the one that works for you.

There is a difference between finishing and completion, two different frequencies, like the radio stations above. Finishing is logistical, while completion is attitudinal. Finishing is a step that comes at the end of a series of actions. Completion is a state of wholeness you enjoy no matter what your state of action. Wholeness is not a goal you achieve at the end of your life. It is an experience you enjoy in the midst of life.

When are you done? Never, and always.

32

ALL READY,
ALREADY

*Do you not say, 'There are yet four months,
then comes the harvest'?
Look, I tell you, lift up your eyes, and see that
the fields are white for harvest now.*

— JOHN 4:35

In Richard Bach's classic parable *Jonathan Livingston Seagull*, the mentor Chiang tells young aspirant Jonathan, "To fly as fast as thought, to anywhere that is . . . you must begin by knowing that you have already arrived." Chiang was teaching that enlightenment and manifestation are a form of reverse engineering. You have to start from where you want to end up.

My friend Sharon's father had a sneaky way of asking his wife for a favor. While the couple sat on their sofa watching television, her dad would turn to her mom and say, "While you're up, would you please get me a soda?" The oddity of the situation was that Mom had indicated no inclination to get up or go anywhere. Yet in Dad's mind, she was already up. Most of the time, Sharon recounted, Dad ended up with a soda.

While feminist readers have already come up with some invigorating responses to Sharon's dad, this example illustrates a principle that can help you manifest what you want. In sales terminology, it's called the "assumed close." You speak to your customer and act as if he or she has already decided to buy your product. In your mind, the sale is already done. While you may not make your sale every time, you will make it more often if you assume it will happen, or has already happened, than if you wonder or worry that it may not.

The assumed close principle goes far beyond sales, and can change your life if you grasp and practice it. It is the secret of all great inventors, teachers, artists, statesmen, heal-

> Imagination is more important than knowledge.
> — Albert Einstein

ers, and visionaries. Anyone who has ever created anything— that's all of us, all the time—has tapped into the *idea* for the creation before the creation came forth. Edison *conceived* of the lightbulb in his mind before it showed up in his laboratory. Einstein *envisioned* a split atom. Gates, Wozniak, and Jobs *imagined* something no one had ever seen—the personal computer. Ideas always precede creation.

To discover is to *dis-cover*—to remove the veil between what is seen and unseen, what has been and what could be. The thing you envision is already so, and you pluck it from universal mind. When the object of your intention becomes sufficiently real in your inner world, you generate the

> The creative is the place where no one else has ever been. . . . You have to leave the city of your comfort and go into the wilderness of your intuition. . . . What you'll discover will be wonderful. What you'll discover will be yourself.
> — Alan Alda

momentum to birth it in the outer world. When someone asked Michelangelo how he sculpted the magnificent statue David, he answered, "I saw David in the stone and chipped away everything that was not David."

When I write a book, I do not feel that I am creating it. On some level the book is already written. My job is to record it as true to the material as possible and bring it to the world. The experience is more like bearing a child than manufacturing a new item.

After my first book was published and I began to present seminars, sponsors would introduce me as an author. I was uncomfortable with that appellation, since I did not feel that I wrote the material. I feel more like a recording secretary than an author. Many artists and inventors recount a similar experience. We are not creators; we are co-creators with a Higher Power.

Everything Is Yours Now

All things that exist, have ever existed, or will exist, exist always. This is so because everything that exists represents an idea, and ideas transcend time and space. Our technology has caught up with this principle. A movie is captured on film and lives digitally on a DVD or storage device practically forever. Even though the movie was made a long time ago, you can pop the disc into your DVD player or download it to your viewer and all the characters, scenes, story lines, and music come to life in your living room. At this moment George Bailey is returning to his family, tears streaming down his cheeks, hugging his wife and kids with an appreciation he has never known before. Ben-Hur is defeating the evil Messala in the famous chariot race as you take your seat in the coliseum to cheer. E.T., about to leave Earth, is touching Elliott on his forehead and assuring him that he'll be right there.

Such events are not simply fictional or historical; they are rooms in a vast mansion, realms of the mind, theaters of the universe you can visit anytime you choose. They are here now and will be always.

Great ideas to be developed in the future are already here for you to reap and harvest. Leonardo da Vinci sketched the submarine and helicopter 400 years before their creation. *Star Trek* prophesied computer floppy disks, cell phones, iPads, phasers (Tasers), "hypospray" hypodermic injections, voice-recognition universal translators, bionic eyes, and MRI-technology tricorders. In a very real sense, the future is already available for those willing to claim it. Your ideal self living your ideal life is not simply a long-range wish or goal. It is already so.

Ripe for Harvest

Although Jesus Christ is regarded primarily as a religious leader, he was more fundamentally a master metaphysician. He achieved miracles because he understood the crucial relationship between mind and matter. He gave many clues that you and I have access to the same power he utilized: "In my Father's house there are many mansions" means that in universal mind all realities or dimensions of experience coexist simultaneously. "The kingdom of God is within you" reminds us that we already own what we seek. Jesus's most mystical yet practical teaching was: "Come; for all things are now ready."

Visionaries see what could be as if it already is. To big-picture thinkers, life is not a competition for limited resources, but a feast from which we select what we prefer. Our human journey is not a dilemma of insufficiency, but an adventure into all-sufficiency. ("I am come that [you] might have life . . . more abundantly" [John 10:10].) There is enough of everything for everyone because the universe is brimming with supply. We just need to open our eyes to broader reality and use it for our highest good.

You have enough already because you are enough already, and you always will be. Your wholeness is not negotiable. It is a fact of life, surer than gravity or the rising of the sun. No matter what you think, say, or do, you cannot add to or diminish your rich and royal self. You can overlook it and live like a pauper, but your true prosperity and power are held in trust for you until you claim them.

That day may be closer than you think—perhaps even today. All the love, life, health, and wealth you value are available beginning right where you stand. They are given freely, and all you need to receive them is to be as generous to yourself as life has been to you. Do not delay joy for want of time, geography, finances, or approval—or any other requirement you have been taught. Teach yourself freedom with the same zeal the world has taught you limits. Do not banish happiness to a future time, and do not consign it to any source outside yourself. There is a room in the universe where all that you seek is already given. Permission to enter is granted.

Acknowledgments

I am deeply grateful to the loving and talented friends and professionals who have supported me and contributed to the content and energy of this book. My heartfelt thanks to:

— My beloved partner Dee, for her boundless belief in me and my work; for her extraordinary beauty, heart, and mind; and for supporting me to focus on the writing and principles this book stands for.

— Kathy McDuff and Rich Lucas, for their quality feedback, assisting to interface with business and personal relationships, and keeping the company running smoothly and efficiently.

— The leaders and staff at Hay House, including Louise L. Hay, founder, visionary, role model, and healer; Reid Tracy, for his impeccable intuition, trust, and relaxed yet efficient helmsmanship; Stacey Smith, efficient angel of support; Alex Freemon, editor who rocks and is a delight to work with; Christy Salinas, for her design supervision; Julie Davison, for her talented graphic design; Riann Bender, for her interior design; and Diane Ray and the entire staff of Hay House Radio, who oversee and engineer my radio show.

— Aziza Seykota, for her brilliant research assistance and feedback.

— Jean Sprague, for her assistance in gathering the statistics on medicine and healing.

— Readers like you, who make it possible for me to do what I love to do the most.

Great Spirit keeps showing up as all of you, and I am deeply grateful.

About the Author

Alan Cohen, M.A., is the author of many popular inspirational books, including the best-selling *The Dragon Doesn't Live Here Anymore* and the award-winning *A Deep Breath of Life*. He is a contributing writer for the #1 *New York Times* best-selling series *Chicken Soup for the Soul,* and his monthly column, "From the Heart," is published in magazines internationally. His work has been featured on CNN and **Oprah.com** and in *USA Today, The Washington Post,* and the book *101 Top Experts.* His books have been translated into 24 foreign languages.

Alan hosts the popular show *Get Real* weekly on Hay House Radio, and he is a featured presenter in the award-winning documentary *Finding Joe,* illuminating the hero's journey depicted by mythologist Joseph Campbell. Alan keynotes and presents seminars in the field of life mastery and vision psychology. He resides with his family in Maui, Hawaii.

Learn More with Alan Cohen

If you have enjoyed and benefitted from *Enough Already*, you may want to deepen your understanding and inspiration by participating in Alan Cohen's in-person seminars, online courses, personal mentorship, or life coach training.

Quote for the Day—An inspirational quotation e-mailed to you each day (free)

Monthly e-Newsletter—Uplifting articles and announcements of events (free)

Wisdom for Today—A stimulating life lesson e-mailed to you daily

Life Mastery Training—A transformational retreat to align your life with your passion, power, and purpose

Life Coach Training—Become a professional life coach or enhance your career with coaching skills

Personal Mentorship—Coaching with Alan, plus online courses and teleseminars

For information on Alan Cohen's books, CDs,
videos, seminars, and online courses, contact:

Website: **www.AlanCohen.com**
E-mail: info@AlanCohen.com
Phone: (800) 568-3079
(808) 572-0001 (outside U.S.)
(808) 575-9111 (fax)

Or write to:

Alan Cohen Programs and Publications
P.O. Box 835
Haiku, HI 96708

NOTES

NOTES

NOTES

NOTES

Hay House Titles of Related Interest

YOU CAN HEAL YOUR LIFE, the movie,
starring Louise L. Hay & Friends
(available as a 1-DVD program and an expanded 2-DVD set)
Watch the trailer at: **www.LouiseHayMovie.com**

THE SHIFT, the movie,
starring Dr. Wayne W. Dyer
(available as a 1-DVD program and an expanded 2-DVD set)
Watch the trailer at: **www.DyerMovie.com**

✧

FINDING OUR WAY HOME:
Heartwarming Stories That Ignite Our Spiritual Core,
by Gerald G. Jampolsky, M.D., and Diane V. Cirincione, Ph.D.

GETTING INTO THE VORTEX:
Guided Meditations CD and User Guide,
by Esther and Jerry Hicks (The Teachings of Abraham®)

LOVE, GOD, AND THE ART OF FRENCH COOKING,
by James F. Twyman

THE MINDFUL MANIFESTO:
How Doing Less and Noticing More Can Help Us Thrive in a
Stressed-Out World, by Dr. Jonty Heaversedge & Ed Halliwell

SHIFT HAPPENS!: How to Live an Inspired Life . . .
Starting Right Now! by Robert Holden, Ph.D.

TRAVELING AT THE SPEED OF LOVE, by Sonia Choquette

YOU CAN CREATE AN EXCEPTIONAL LIFE,
by Louise Hay and Cheryl Richardson

All of the above are available at your local bookstore,
or may be ordered by contacting Hay House (see next page).

✧

We hope you enjoyed this Hay House book. If you'd like to receive our online catalog featuring additional information on Hay House books and products, or if you'd like to find out more about the Hay Foundation, please contact:

Hay House, Inc., P.O. Box 5100, Carlsbad, CA 92018-5100
(760) 431-7695 or (800) 654-5126
(760) 431-6948 (fax) or (800) 650-5115 (fax)
www.hayhouse.com® • **www.hayfoundation.org**

Published and distributed in Australia by:
Hay House Australia Pty. Ltd., 18/36 Ralph St., Alexandria NSW 2015 •
Phone: 612-9669-4299 • *Fax:* 612-9669-4144 • www.hayhouse.com.au

Published and distributed in the United Kingdom by:
Hay House UK, Ltd., 292B Kensal Rd., London W10 5BE • *Phone:*
44-20-8962-1230 • *Fax:* 44-20-8962-1239 • www.hayhouse.co.uk

Published and distributed in the Republic of South Africa by:
Hay House SA (Pty), Ltd., P.O. Box 990, Witkoppen 2068 •
Phone/Fax: 27-11-467-8904 • www.hayhouse.co.za

Published in India by: Hay House Publishers India,
Muskaan Complex, Plot No. 3, B-2, Vasant Kunj, New Delhi 110 070 •
Phone: 91-11-4176-1620 • *Fax:* 91-11-4176-1630 • www.hayhouse.co.in

Distributed in Canada by:
Raincoast, 9050 Shaughnessy St., Vancouver, B.C. V6P 6E5 •
Phone: (604) 323-7100 • *Fax:* (604) 323-2600 • www.raincoast.com

---

Take Your Soul on a Vacation

Visit **www.HealYourLife.com**® to regroup, recharge, and reconnect with your own magnificence.

Featuring blogs, mind-body-spirit news, and life-changing wisdom from Louise Hay and friends.

Visit **www.HealYourLife.com** today!